MILOS GR_____ TRAVEL GUIDE 2023 2024

Discovering Milos: A Comprehensive Travel Guide to Greece Hidden Gem

Island King J

Welcome to Milos Greece

As the ferry gently glided into the picturesque harbor of Milos, Greece, I couldn't help but feel a sense of anticipation. The island's reputation for stunning landscapes, crystal-clear waters, and rich cultural heritage had drawn me in, and now I was finally here. With a deep breath, I stepped ashore, ready to embark on an unforgettable journey.

My first destination was the enchanting village of Plaka, nestled atop a hill overlooking the island. Cobblestone streets meandered through narrow alleyways lined with vibrant bougainvillea and traditional whitewashed houses. Plaka offered breathtaking panoramic views of the Aegean Sea, creating a picturesque backdrop for exploration. I visited the Panagia Korfiatissa, a striking Byzantine church that stood proudly at the highest point of Plaka. Inside, its walls adorned with beautiful frescoes, I marveled at the spiritual aura that filled the space. From there, I wandered through the maze-like streets, stumbling upon charming local shops selling handmade ceramics and delicate lace.

Eager to indulge in the island's renowned beaches, I embarked on a quest to explore its coastline. My first stop was Sarakiniko Beach, a unique lunar landscape crafted by volcanic activity. I marveled at the dazzling white volcanic rocks contrasting with the deep blue sea, creating a surreal ambiance that seemed otherworldly. Next, I ventured to the remote Tsigrado Beach, accessible only by descending a steep cliff with the aid of a rope ladder. Once there, I reveled in the seclusion and tranquility of this hidden gem, as if I had stumbled upon my own private paradise.

No exploration of Milos would be complete without a visit to its ancient sites. The island is renowned for its archaeological wealth, and I was eager to uncover its secrets. In the village of Tripiti, I wandered through the ruins of the ancient theater, imagining the vibrant performances that once took place against the backdrop of the Aegean Sea. At the Catacombs of Milos, I delved into the island's early Christian history. The underground network of tunnels and chambers, carved into the volcanic rock, served as a burial site and later became a place of worship. The atmosphere was solemn yet captivating, transporting me back in time.

No travel experience is complete without savoring the local cuisine, and Milos did not disappoint. I immersed myself in the island's gastronomic offerings, delighting in fresh seafood, flavorful olives, and creamy cheese. The quaint tavernas of Adamas and Pollonia became my go-to spots, where I relished in the warm hospitality of the locals and indulged in mouthwatering dishes.

As the sun began to set on my final day in Milos, I found myself reflecting on the memories I had made. From the ethereal beauty of its beaches to the rich tapestry of its history and culture, the island had captured my heart. I bid farewell to the warm embrace of its people and the idyllic landscapes that had left an indelible mark on my soul.

My journey through Milos, Greece, had been nothing short of a transformative experience. I immersed myself in the island's beauty, ventured into its ancient past, and savored the flavors of its culinary traditions. As I boarded the ferry back to the mainland, I carried with me the enchantment of Milos, forever etched in my memories, longing for the day when I would return to its shores once again.

15 reasons why Milos should be your next tourist destination

1. Breathtaking Beaches: Milos boasts some of the most stunning beaches in Greece, with their pristine white sands, crystal-clear turquoise waters, and unique rock formations. Each beach offers a distinct ambiance, from the secluded coves of Tsigrado to the ethereal beauty of Sarakiniko. Prepare to be mesmerized.

2. Secluded Paradise: Milos is a haven for those seeking tranquility and seclusion. Unlike its more popular neighbors, the island remains relatively undiscovered by mass tourism, allowing you to immerse yourself in a serene and peaceful atmosphere, far away from the crowds.

3. Quaint Village Charm: The traditional villages of Milos, such as Plaka and Pollonia, exude a captivating charm. Wander through narrow streets lined with whitewashed houses adorned with vibrant bougainvillea, and lose yourself in the enchanting ambiance that harks back to a simpler time.

4. Cultural Heritage: Milos is a treasure trove of ancient history and archaeological sites. Explore the ruins of the ancient theater in Tripiti, visit the Catacombs of Milos, and witness the island's rich past come alive. The layers of history will ignite your imagination and deepen your appreciation for this remarkable destination.

5. Spectacular Sunsets: Milos offers some of the most breathtaking sunsets in the Aegean Sea. Whether you're perched on a cliff overlooking the sea or lounging on a tranquil beach, watching the sun dip below the horizon in a blaze of vibrant colors will leave you awestruck and create memories that will last a lifetime.

6. Delectable Cuisine: Indulge your taste buds in Milos' culinary delights. From fresh seafood caught daily to traditional Greek dishes bursting with flavor, the island's tavernas and restaurants will take you on a gastronomic journey. Savor each bite while enjoying the warm hospitality of the locals.

7. Volcanic Wonders: Milos' volcanic origins have gifted the island with unique geological formations. Explore the lunar landscape of Sarakiniko, hike to the top of Profitis Ilias to witness the volcanic caldera, or bathe in the hot springs of Paleochori. Nature enthusiasts and geology buffs will be enthralled by the island's natural wonders.

8. Unforgettable Boat Tours: Embark on a boat tour around Milos and discover hidden coves, sea caves, and secluded beaches accessible only by sea. Sail along the rugged coastline, swim in crystalline waters, and create cherished memories as you explore the island's breathtaking shores from a different perspective.

9. Warm Greek Hospitality: Milos is renowned for its warm and welcoming locals. Prepare to be embraced by their genuine hospitality, as they share their island's treasures and traditions with open arms. The genuine kindness and friendliness of the people will make your stay in Milos even more heartwarming.

10. Captivating Sunrises: Start your day with a magical sunrise experience in Milos. Find a peaceful spot to witness the dawn break over the azure sea, painting the sky in hues of pink and gold. The tranquil beauty of the early morning will fill your heart with serenity and set the tone for a remarkable day ahead.

11. Diverse Activities: Milos offers a wide range of activities to suit every traveler's taste. Whether you're an avid hiker, a water sports enthusiast, a history buff, or an art lover, you'll find an array of options to keep you engaged and entertained throughout your stay.

12. Postcard-Worthy Scenery: Milos is a photographer's paradise, with picture-perfect landscapes at every turn. From the colorful fishing boats bobbing in the

 harbor to the breathtaking panoramas from hilltop villages, the island provides endless opportunities to capture the beauty of Greece in all its glory.

13. Unspoiled Nature: Milos is blessed with unspoiled natural beauty, offering a peaceful sanctuary for nature lovers. Explore its rugged coastline, hike through scenic trails, and encounter rare flora and fauna that thrive in this untouched paradise. Immerse yourself in nature and reconnect with the world around you.

14. Authentic Greek Island Experience: Milos embodies the essence of a traditional Greek island, where old-world charm merges seamlessly with natural wonders. Experience the genuine local culture, witness traditional festivities, and embrace the unhurried pace of life that defines the Greek island way.

15. Lasting Memories: Above all, a vacation in Milos promises to create lasting memories that will forever hold a special place in your heart. The island's captivating beauty, warm hospitality, and unforgettable experiences will leave an indelible mark, ensuring that Milos remains a cherished part of your travel journey.

So, pack your bags, immerse yourself in the heartwarming embrace of Milos, and embark on an extraordinary adventure that will leave you with treasured moments and a longing to return again and again.

Introduction

Welcome to the enchanting island of Milos, Greece—a hidden gem nestled in the heart of the Aegean Sea. With its captivating beauty, rich cultural heritage, and pristine beaches, Milos beckons travelers seeking an authentic and unforgettable Greek island experience. This travel guide is your gateway to discovering the hidden treasures, heartwarming experiences, and breathtaking landscapes that await you on this captivating island.

In these pages, you will embark on a journey that will take you through the maze-like streets of the traditional villages, where whitewashed houses adorned with bougainvillea create a postcard-worthy setting. You will explore the island's ancient history, tracing the footsteps of ancient civilizations at archaeological sites such as the Catacombs of Milos and the ancient theater in Tripiti. And you will indulge your senses in the gastronomic delights of Milos, savoring the flavors of freshly caught seafood and local specialties that will leave an everlasting impression.

The pristine beaches of Milos will entice you to unwind and soak in the beauty of their turquoise waters and dramatic rock formations. From the lunar landscape of Sarakiniko to the hidden coves of Tsigrado, each beach offers a unique experience, inviting you to relax, swim, and bask in the Mediterranean sun.

But Milos is not just about natural beauty—it is also about the warmth and hospitality of its people. Throughout your journey, you will encounter the genuine kindness and friendliness of the locals, who will make you feel like a welcomed guest in their island paradise.

This travel guide will serve as your companion, providing you with essential information, insider tips, and suggested itineraries to make the most of your time in Milos. Whether you're a history enthusiast, a nature lover, or simply seeking a tranquil escape, there is something here for every traveler.

So, join us as we explore the cobblestone streets, dive into the Aegean Sea, savor the local cuisine, and immerse ourselves in the heartwarming embrace of Milos. Let this guide be your passport to uncovering the hidden gems, creating unforgettable memories, and falling in love with the timeless allure of this captivating Greek island.

Are you ready to embark on this extraordinary journey? Let's dive into the wonders of Milos together.

CHAPTER ONE
Getting To Know Milos
Geographical and Climate

Milos is a volcanic island in Greece's Cyclades archipelago known for its distinctive geological structures and magnificent sceneries. The island is around 151 square kilometers (58 square miles) in size and is distinguished by a diversified landscape that includes steep cliffs and volcanic beaches, as well as gentle hills and lush valleys.

Milos' unusual look is due to its volcanic history. Volcanic activity has sculpted the island's topography, resulting in magnificent rock formations like as pumice cliffs, volcanic ash deposits, and jagged coasts. Sarakiniko, one of the island's most renowned beaches, is distinguished by its lunar-like white volcanic rocks, which create an unearthly atmosphere.

The island also has numerous attractive settlements, notably the quaint Plaka, located on a mountain, and Pollonia, a fishing community. These historic communities include whitewashed cottages with colorful doors and windows, tiny cobblestone walkways, and breathtaking views of the Aegean Sea.

Weather and Climate Conditions

Milos has a Mediterranean climate, with hot, dry summers and warm, rainy winters. The weather on the island is affected by its closeness to the sea, with the Aegean Sea cooling temperatures.

Summer in Milos is hot and sunny, with temperatures ranging from 25 to 35 degrees Celsius (77 to 95 degrees Fahrenheit). A soft wind blows over the island, providing some reprieve from the heat. It's the ideal time to explore the island's gorgeous beaches and outdoor activities.

Milos is best visited in the spring (April to May) and fall (September to October), when temperatures range from 18 to 25 degrees Celsius (64 to 77 degrees Fahrenheit). These seasons provide nice weather for touring the island, with flowering wildflowers giving splashes of color to the scenery.

Winter (December to February) is the off-season for visitors to Milos. Temperatures on the island range from 10 to 15 degrees Celsius (50 to 59 degrees Fahrenheit). While it may rain on occasion, the winters are typically moderate in comparison to other parts of Greece. Despite the calmer mood, visiting Milos during the winter enables you to see a different aspect of the island and appreciate its tranquil beauty.

Natural disasters

Milos, like other volcanic islands, has the potential for volcanic activity. While the island's volcanic past adds to its attractiveness, it's crucial to remember that volcanic outbursts are uncommon and infrequent. Milos' last volcanic activity occurred thousands of years ago, and the island is now considered inactive.

Milos, like any other coastal location, is prone to earthquakes. These earthquakes, however, are normally of low to moderate strength and pose little danger to tourists. The island is well-prepared for such disasters, and the infrastructure is designed to resist earthquakes.

To guarantee your safety during your vacation to Milos, it is essential to be updated about local weather conditions and to follow any advice or suggestions issued by local authorities.

Finally, the volcanic origins of Milos have resulted in spectacular landscapes and distinctive rock formations. The Mediterranean environment of the island offers pleasant summers and moderate winters, making it an appealing resort all year. While volcanic activity and earthquakes have occurred on Milos, the island is deemed inactive and takes the appropriate safeguards to protect the safety of its citizens and tourists.

History

Milos has a long history, extending back thousands of years, with traces of human occupancy reaching back to the Neolithic era. The island's strategic position in the Aegean Sea, as well as its abundant natural resources, made it an appealing destination for numerous ancient civilizations, leaving behind a tapestry of cultural history that enchants tourists even now.

Prehistoric Period

Milos was an important part of the Cycladic civilization throughout the ancient age. Excavations in the Phylakopi region have uncovered the ruins of a flourishing Bronze Age community that flourished between the third and second millennia BCE. The Phylakopi civilization participated in commerce, pottery manufacture, and agriculture, leaving behind exquisite ceramics, figures, and objects that provide details about their everyday life.

Classical Era

Milos became a member of the Athenian Empire throughout the Classical era and experienced prosperity. The famed white marble quarries of the island, notably the Aphrodite of Milos (Venus de Milo), were recognized throughout the ancient world for their high-quality marble. The statue, unearthed on the island in 1820, is currently placed in Paris's Louvre Museum and has become an iconic emblem of ancient Greek art.

The Hellenistic and Roman eras

During the Hellenistic era, Milos grew in importance as a trading and commercial city. The island's strategic position along trade routes drew the attention of several countries, notably the Macedonians and the Egyptian Ptolemies. Milos was soon absorbed into the Roman Empire's enormous boundaries, and the island prospered as a center for agricultural, commercial, and nautical operations.

Early Christian and Byzantine Periods
Milos became an important location for early Christian communities as Christianity spread. The Catacombs of Milos, in the town of Tripiti, were used as a burial ground for early Christians before being converted into places of worship. These subterranean chambers cut into the volcanic rock give testament to the island's early Christian history and are an important archaeological site to investigate.

Venetian and Ottoman Rule
Milos was ruled by the Venetians and the Ottomans alternately throughout the medieval era. Recognizing the island's strategic significance, the Venetians fortified its capital, Plaka, and built defensive fortifications that may still be seen today. Milos was eventually taken over by the Ottoman Empire, and the island became part of its maritime empire, adding to the region's trade and cultural interactions.

Modern Era
During the Greek War of freedom in the early nineteenth century, Milos, like the rest of Greece, battled for freedom. Local Milotians enthusiastically participated in the battle for independence on the island, which played a role in the revolution. Milos underwent a period of prosperity and development after Greece's independence, embracing modernisation while conserving its own cultural history.

Milos is now a popular tourist destination, attracting tourists from all over the globe with its beautiful beaches, volcanic scenery, and rich history. Visitors may immerse themselves in the intriguing trip through time by visiting the island's historical landmarks, museums, and archaeological riches.

Milos' layers of history will be revealed as you travel the island, from ancient remains to medieval defenses, Byzantine churches to tiny rural towns. Every step you take on this remarkable island will be a monument to the continuing heritage of the civilizations that created its identity.

Demography and Culture

Culture

Milos has a thriving and diverse cultural history that is profoundly based in its historical and geographic influences. The culture of the island is a synthesis of ancient Greek traditions, Byzantine influences, and the distinct traits of the Cycladic islands.

Music, dancing, and traditional festivities are all important parts of Milos' cultural fabric. Folklore dances like the Ballos and the Sirto are performed during festivals and local gatherings. These energetic dances demonstrate the islanders' love of their cultural heritage while also providing a glimpse into Milos' traditional music and dance traditions.

Milos' indigenous food reflects the island's cultural uniqueness. Milos' cuisine, influenced by the island's geographical position and agricultural resources, emphasizes fresh fish, locally produced products, and classic Greek recipes. Don't miss out on delectable delicacies like octopus stew, sun-dried tomatoes, and local cheese variations like xinotyro and kopanisti.

Milos offers a variety of cultural events and festivals throughout the year to commemorate its history, arts, and customs. The Cultural Summer Festival, hosted at Milos' old theater, features theatrical performances, concerts, and art exhibits that draw artists and viewers from all across Greece.

Demographics

Milos has a population of around 5,000 people, most of whom live in the island's principal villages such as Adamas, Plaka, and

Pollonia. The island's natural resources and breathtaking scenery shape the way of life of the local people, who mostly engaged in agricultural, fishing, and tourism-related businesses.

The Milotian people's friendly and inviting disposition is a distinguishing feature of the island's demographics. guests to Milos will be greeted with true kindness and friendliness by the residents, who take delight in sharing the riches and cultural legacy of their island with guests.

Milos is also a popular location for overseas people who have decided to live on the island. Many expatriates have been lured to the island's natural beauty, calm lifestyle, and close-knit society, contributing to cultural variety and establishing a dynamic international community.

You will get the chance to connect with people, immerse yourself in their rituals, and observe their real pride in their cultural heritage as a tourist to Milos. From vibrant chats at a local taverna to traditional events, you will definitely experience the warmth and friendliness that distinguish the people of Milos.

Milos' distinct combination of cultural traditions, friendly locals, and varied demographics make it a perfect destination for visitors looking for a genuine Greek island experience. As you discover the cultural tapestry that makes Milos really unique, seize the chance to engage with the local people, learn about their traditions, and create memorable memories.

CHAPTER TWO
Making Travel Plans
Best time to visit

Milos is a lovely Greek island that provides a great experience all year. Choosing the perfect time to visit, on the other hand, may substantially improve your vacation and guarantee you make the most of your stay. What you need to know about the ideal time to visit Milos is as follows:

1. Spring (April to May): One of the greatest seasons to visit Milos is in the spring. With temperatures ranging from 18 to 25 degrees Celsius (64 to 77 degrees Fahrenheit), the weather is lovely. The island is lush and full of wildflowers, making for a gorgeous environment. In addition, compared to the peak summer season, spring provides fewer people, enabling you to enjoy the island's attractions and beaches more pleasantly.

2. Summer (June to August): For good reason, summer is the busiest tourist season in Milos. With temperatures ranging from 25 to 35 degrees Celsius (77 to 95 degrees Fahrenheit), the weather is pleasant and bright. This is the ideal time to relax on the island's magnificent beaches, swim in the crystal-clear seas, and participate in a variety of water sports. The island comes alive with a bustling atmosphere, with restaurants, beach bars, and stores open for business. Keep in mind, however, that the island might be congested during this season, particularly in July and August.

3. Autumn (September to October): Another fantastic season to explore Milos. Temperatures are nice, ranging from 18 to 25 degrees Celsius (64 to 77 degrees Fahrenheit). Summer crowds start to thin out, making for a more quiet and relaxing experience. You may still enjoy the beaches, see the sites, and participate in outdoor activities. Autumn also provides the chance to see breathtaking sunsets and take advantage of decreased lodging expenses.

4. Winter (December to February): Winter is Milos' low season. The island retains its attractiveness and peacefulness despite the lower temperature, which ranges from 10 to 15 degrees Celsius (50 to 59 degrees Fahrenheit). Winter is an excellent season to visit if you want to relax and see the island's unique native life. The environment is calm, and you'll be able to interact with friendly people while admiring the island's natural beauty away from the masses. Please keep in mind that certain businesses and tourist attractions may have modified their operation hours during this time.

Finally, the optimum time to visit Milos is determined by your own interests and the kind of experience you desire. Milos will fascinate you with its gorgeous scenery, stunning beaches, and friendly hospitality, whether you prefer the bustling ambiance of summer or the calm and quiet of the off-season.

Visa and Travel Document Requirements

When planning a vacation to Milos, Greece, make sure you have all of the relevant travel papers and understand the visa requirements. Here's what you should know:

1. Passport: Make sure your passport is valid for at least six months beyond the date you want to leave Greece. Before flying, check your passport's expiry date and, if required, renew it.

2. Visa Requirements: Because Greece is a member of the Schengen Area, travelers from numerous countries may enter the country without a visa for short stays (up to 90 days) for tourist, business, or family visits. Visa requirements, however, differ depending on your nationality. With a valid passport or national ID card, citizens of the European Union (EU), European Economic Area (EEA), and Switzerland may enter Greece.

3. Visa-Free Countries: Citizens of various countries, including the United States, Canada, Australia, New Zealand, Japan, South Korea, and others, may visit Greece without a visa for up to 90 days during a 180-day period. This includes tourism and various other non-work-related activities. Before going, be sure to verify the visa requirements for your place of citizenship.

4. Visa-on-arrival: Some non-visa-exempt nations may be eligible for a visa-on-arrival while entering Greece. This enables you to get a visa for a charge at the point of entry, such as Athens International Airport or the ports on Milos. However, it is best to clarify the most recent visa requirements and processes with the Greek embassy or consulate in your home country.

5. Longer Stays: If you want to remain in Greece for more than 90 days or to participate in activities such as a job or study, you will almost certainly need to apply for a visa ahead of time. You may need to get a long-term visa or a resident permit depending on the purpose of your stay.

6. Travel Insurance: Travel insurance that covers medical expenditures, trip cancellation or interruption, and loss or theft of personal possessions is strongly recommended. Check with your insurance company to be sure you have enough coverage for your trip to Milos.

7. Customs and Entry Requirements: You may be needed to go through customs and submit information about the purpose and length of your stay while entering Greece. Supporting documentation, such as hotel reservations, return airline tickets, and confirmation of adequate finances for your stay, should be readily accessible if immigration authorities require them.

Before your journey, be sure to check the latest travel warnings and entry requirements from your home country's government and the Greek embassy or consulate. This ensures that you have the most up-to-date information on travel papers and visa requirements for your trip to Milos, Greece.

Currency and Exchange Rates

When planning a vacation to Milos, it's essential to understand the local currency and the conversion rates. Everything you need to know about money and exchange rates in Milos, Greece is right here:

1. The Euro (€) is the official currency of Greece. It is the sole currency accepted across the nation, including Milos. Carry enough cash in Euros for minor transactions, since some businesses may not take credit cards for small purchases or in isolated locations.

2. ATMs: ATMs (Automated Teller Machines) are accessible in the major towns of Milos, including Adamas, Plaka, and Pollonia. The most convenient method to withdraw cash in the local currency is via ATMs. They accept Visa, Mastercard, and Maestro, as well as major foreign debit and credit cards. Some ATMs may charge a fee for withdrawals, so check with your bank to see if there are any extra fees.

3. Credit cards are generally accepted in Milos, particularly at bigger places including as hotels, restaurants, and stores. Although Visa and Mastercard are the most often accepted cards, it's always a good idea to have some cash on hand for smaller companies or establishments that only take cash payments.

4. Exchange Rates: Exchange rates vary on a daily basis, so it's important to remain up to date to guarantee you obtain the best prices for your money. Banks, exchange offices, and ATMs may have somewhat different exchange rates. Banks often provide cheap rates, however their hours of operation may be restricted. Compare rates and think about converting a modest quantity of cash for urgent needs upon arrival.

5. Currency Exchange: Major banks and exchange offices in Milos provide currency exchange services. Banks often provide higher rates than exchange offices, although their hours of operation may be restricted, particularly on weekends and holidays. Exchange offices may be located in tourist destinations and operate on a more flexible schedule, including weekends.

6. Foreign money: It is normally advised to convert your local money for Euros before arriving in Milos. If you are unable to do so, significant currencies such as US dollars or British pounds may be exchanged through banks or exchange offices. Keep in mind that non-Euro currency conversion rates may not be as beneficial.

7. Currency Conversion applications: To get real-time exchange rates, consider utilizing currency conversion applications or websites. This will allow you to keep track of current rates and more precisely forecast spending.

8. Tipping: Tipping is not appreciated in Greece, however, it is appreciated for excellent service. In restaurants, a tip of 5% to 10% of the entire bill is customary. You may round up or offer a larger tip for excellent service. Tipping hotel personnel, tour guides, and taxi drivers is also expected if you are pleased with their services.

Remember to notify your bank or credit card issuer of your trip intentions to Greece in order to prevent problems with card use. Having a mix of cash and credit cards will give you more options throughout your stay to Milos.

How to Get to Milos

Milos, situated in Greece's Cyclades archipelago, has a variety of transportation alternatives for getting to the island. Whether you choose to travel by air or water, there are simple and dependable solutions accessible.

By Air

Milos Island National Airport (MLO) is the island's major airport. Here's everything you need to know about flying to Milos:

- **Domestic Flights:** Milos is well-connected to Athens, Greece's capital, by frequent domestic flights. Daily flights between Athens International Airport (ATH) and Milos Island National Airport are operated by many carriers, including Olympic Air and Aegean carriers. The trip takes around 30 to 40 minutes, making it a speedy and comfortable method to go to the island.

- **International Flights:** During the peak summer season, Milos may also receive a limited number of international flights from select European cities. It's advisable to check with airlines or travel agencies for any direct or seasonal international flights to Milos.

- **Airport Facilities**: Milos Island National Airport is a small airport with basic facilities. It has a café and a small souvenir shop. Car rental agencies are available at the airport if you wish to rent a vehicle for transportation during your stay.

By Sea

Regular ferry services link Milos to other Greek islands and mainland ports. The following are the most important things to know when getting to Milos by sea:

- **Ferry Services:** Ferries are a popular and picturesque way to get to Milos. Regular ferry connections are available from Athens' ports of Piraeus and Rafina, as well as from other Cycladic islands like Santorini, Mykonos, and Paros. Blue Star Ferries, Hellenic Seaways, and SeaJets offer ferry services to and from Milos. The length of the boat ride is determined on the route and might vary from 2 to 7 hours depending on the distance.

- High-Speed Ferries: For speedier transit to Milos, high-speed catamarans and hydrofoils are available. These boats provide faster transit times than traditional ferries but may have restricted car capacity. High-speed ferry services are highly popular during the summer season, so plan ahead of time, especially if you're going with a car.

- Port of Adamas: The primary port of Milos is Adamas, which is situated on the island's northeastern shore. Upon arrival, you will discover a variety of facilities and services, such as ticket offices, vehicle rental companies, taxi stands, and bus stations. Adamas is also the island's main center for local transportation.

How to Get Around Milos

When you arrive in Milos, you'll discover a variety of transportation choices to help you explore the island and get about easily throughout your visit. Milos has the following local transportation options:

1. Rental Cars, Scooters, and ATVs: Renting a vehicle, scooter, or ATV is a popular and simple way to explore Milos. Car rental businesses may be found at Adamas, Pollonia, and other tourist spots. Renting a car allows you to explore the island at your own leisure, visit secluded beaches, and find hidden beauties. Before hiring a car, make sure you have a valid driver's license and are acquainted with local traffic laws. Check the rental agreement for details like insurance coverage, fuel policy, and any extra costs.

2. Local buses: Local buses link the major communities, prominent beaches, and tourist sites on Milos. The primary bus station is in downtown Adamas, and buses run on set routes throughout the day. Bus lines serve important places such as Pollonia, Plaka, Sarakiniko Beach, and others. Bus timetables may change depending on the season, so it's best to double-check the schedule ahead of time. The bus system is an inexpensive and environmentally friendly way to go about the island.

3. Taxis: Taxis may be obtained at authorized taxi stops or hailed on the streets of Milos. You may also use the phone numbers offered by hotels or local restaurants to pre-book a cab. Taxis provide convenience and comfort, especially for shorter trips or time-sensitive transfers. To guarantee fair pricing, enquire about the charges and request that the driver use the meter. It's best to reserve a cab in advance during high tourist season, particularly for airport or port trips.

4. Walking and Cycling: Milos is a tiny island with magnificent scenery that is excellent for exploring on foot. The island has beautiful walking routes that lead to breathtaking views, hidden coves, and ancient sites. Walking enables you to immerse yourself in Milos' natural beauty and explore secret nooks at your own speed. Cycling is also a popular mode of transportation, and rental companies lend out bicycles. Walking or cycling about Milos enables you to connect with the island's beauty and enjoy its tranquil ambiance.

When selecting on the best means of transportation for your stay in Milos, keep your tastes, budget, and itinerary in mind. Renting a car gives flexibility and convenience, whilst buses provide affordability and set itineraries. Taxis are a dependable alternative for shorter excursions or transfers while walking or cycling enabling you to get up close and personal with the island's stunning magnificence. Choose the mode of transportation that best suits your travel style, enabling you to make the most of your stay on this enthralling Greek island.

Accommodation Recommendations

Milos offers a wide range of lodging alternatives to accommodate a wide range of interests, budgets, and travel types. Here are three major types of lodging options, with examples for each.

Luxury accommodations

Milos has various magnificent hotels and resorts that provide great facilities, world-class service, and breathtaking views. The 5-star Milos Cove, Santa Maria Luxury Suites & Spa, and Salt Suites & Executive Rooms are a few examples.

1. Cove of Milos

- Location: Milos Cove is situated near Agia Kiriaki, a picturesque town overlooking the Aegean Sea. It is located on Milos' southern shore, with spectacular views of the turquoise ocean and adjacent rocks.

- Convenient Location to major sites: Milos Cove is perfectly positioned near major sites like as Sarakiniko Beach, Firiplaka Beach, and the Milos Catacombs. Pollonia, a lovely hamlet, is just a short drive away.

- Special Features and Services: Milos Cove offers magnificent and large rooms with private balconies or patios, as well as private plunge pools in certain cases. The resort has a beautiful infinity pool, a spa that offers revitalizing treatments, and a gourmet restaurant that serves wonderful Greek and foreign cuisine.

- staying Costs: The cost of staying at Milos Cove varies from $400 to $800 per night, depending on the suite style and season.

2. Santa Maria Luxury Suites & Spa

- Location: Santa Maria Luxury Suites & Spa is located in Adamas, a lovely town near Milos' harbor. It is close to the busy town core and its facilities.

- Convenience to Major Attractions: The hotel is within walking distance to Adamas Beach as well as the town's restaurants, shopping, and nightlife. It is also close to major sights like as Plaka, the Catacombs of Milos, and the Ancient Theater.

Santa Maria Luxury rooms & Spa provides attractively constructed rooms with contemporary conveniences and own balconies or patios. The hotel has a spa and wellness center, an outdoor swimming pool, a fitness facility, and a Mediterranean restaurant. Views of Adamas Bay and the surrounding region are available to guests.

- staying Costs: The projected cost of staying at Santa Maria Luxury Suites & Spa varies from $200 to $400 per night, depending on room style and season.

Salt Suites & Executive Rooms

- Location: Salt Suites & Executive Rooms is in Pollonia, a lovely fishing hamlet on Milos' northeastern coast. It provides a calm environment with stunning views of the Aegean Sea.

- Proximity to Major Attractions: The hotel is only a few steps from Pollonia's beach, providing quick access to swimming, sunbathing, and water sports. It is also ideally located among the village's famous restaurants, cafés, and shopping.

Salt Suites & Executive Rooms provides beautiful and comfortable suites with contemporary facilities and private balconies. Some rooms include private plunge pools or outdoor hot tubs. The hotel serves a continental breakfast and includes a lounge area where visitors may relax and take in the scenery.

- staying Costs: The anticipated cost of staying at Salt Suites & Executive Rooms varies from $150 to $300 per night, depending on suite style and season.

Boutique Inns:
Psaravolada Beach Resort:

- Location: The Psaravolada Resort is located on Milos' southwest shore, overlooking the Aegean Sea. It lies in Agia Kyriaki, a peaceful location famed for its gorgeous beaches and pure seas.

- Proximity to Major Attractions: The resort is adjacent to major attractions like as Sarakiniko Beach, Firiplaka Beach, and the Milos Catacombs. Adamas, a busy hamlet, is just a short drive away.

Psaravolada Resort provides attractively constructed rooms and suites, some with own balconies or verandas overlooking the sea. The resort has a pool, a poolside bar, a restaurant serving Mediterranean cuisine, and a spa with a variety of treatments and massages.

- staying Costs: The projected cost of staying at Psaravolada Resort varies from $200 to $400 per night, depending on room type and season.

Hotel Portiani

- Location: Hotel Portiani lies in the middle of Adamas, Milos' principal harbor. It provides easy access to the harbor, stores, restaurants, and other local facilities.

- Proximity to Major Attractions: Adamas Beach and the town's lively promenade are both within walking distance of the hotel. It's also close to major sights including Plaka, the Catacombs of Milos, and the Ancient Theater.

- Unique Features and Services: Hotel Portiani has pleasant rooms with contemporary conveniences, some of which have balconies or patios. The hotel offers a continental breakfast, a comfortable lounge area, and a rooftop terrace with views of the harbor and the Aegean Sea.

- staying Costs: The projected cost of staying at Hotel Portiani varies from $100 to $200 per night, depending on the room type and season.

Melian Boutique Hotel & Spa

- Location: Melian Boutique Hotel & Spa is situated in Pollonia, a lovely hamlet on Milos' northeastern shore. It provides a serene environment with stunning views of the Aegean Sea and the surrounding island of Kimolos.

- Convenience to Major Attractions: The hotel is a short walk from Pollonia Beach and is surrounded by notable restaurants, cafés, and shopping. It is also close to other attractions including Papafragas Beach and the Folklore and Maritime Museum.

- Unique Features and Services: The Melian Boutique Hotel & Spa has attractively constructed rooms and suites, some of which have own balconies or outdoor hot tubs. There is a spa and wellness center, an outdoor pool, a restaurant offering Greek and Mediterranean cuisine, and a bar at the hotel.

- staying Costs: The expected cost of staying at Melian Boutique Hotel & Spa varies from $200 to $400 per night, depending on room type and season.

Traditional Villas
Medusa Hotel

- Location: Medusa Resort is positioned on a mountaintop overlooking the Aegean Sea in the charming hamlet of Plaka. It has magnificent views and a tranquil ambiance.

- Proximity to Major Attractions: The resort is located within walking distance to Plaka's lovely lanes, shops, and restaurants. It's also close to major sights including the Catacombs of Milos, the Ancient Theater, and Sarakiniko Beach.

- Unique Features and Services: Medusa Resort provides classic Cycladic-style villas with contemporary conveniences, private patios, and breathtaking sea views. The resort has a swimming pool, a poolside bar, and a garden where guests may rest and unwind.

- staying Costs: The anticipated cost of staying at Medusa Resort varies from $200 to $400 per night, depending on the villa type and season.

Sunset Studios Nefeli

- Location: Nefeli Sunset Studios is in Pollonia, a community famed for its spectacular sunsets and laid-back vibe. It is close to the beach and has easy access to local facilities.

- proximity to Major Attractions: The apartments are near Pollonia Beach and within walking distance of the village's restaurants, cafés, and stores. Popular neighboring sites include Papafragas Beach and the Folklore and Maritime Museum.

- Special Features and Services: Nefeli Sunset apartments offers comfortable and well-equipped apartments with own balconies or patios, some of which have sea views. The apartments provide a pleasant and convenient accommodation for visitors to Milos.

  - staying Costs: The projected cost of staying at Nefeli Sunset Studios is between $100 and $200 per night, depending on the studio type and season.

Lagada Beach Hotel

- Location: The Lagada Beach Hotel is situated in Adamas hamlet, with direct access to a sandy beach and stunning views of the Aegean Sea. It is ideally located near the town center and the harbor.

- Proximity to Major Attractions: The hotel is a short walk from Adamas Beach and the town's facilities. It is also near to the Church of Agios Haralambos, the Milos Mining Museum, and the Ecclesiastical Museum.

- Unique Features and Services: The Lagada Beach Hotel offers pleasant rooms and suites, some of which have balconies or patios overlooking the sea. The hotel has a beachside bar, a restaurant that serves Greek and foreign cuisine, and a sun deck where guests may unwind.

- staying Costs: The projected cost of staying at Lagada Beach Hotel varies from $150 to $300 per night, depending on room type and season.

Mid-range accommodation options
Suites by Miland
- Location: Miland Suites is near the hamlet of Adamas, Milos' principal harbor. It is strategically located in the town center, making it simple to reach stores, restaurants, and other services.

- Proximity to Major Attractions: Adamas Beach and the lively promenade are both within walking distance of the hotel. It's also close to major sights including Plaka, the Catacombs of Milos, and the Ancient Theater.

Miland Suites offers big and contemporary suites with separate bedrooms, sitting spaces, and fully outfitted kitchens. Private balconies or patios with views of the sea or the garden are available in certain suites. There is a swimming pool, a children's pool, a playground, and a snack bar at the hotel.

- staying Costs: The projected cost of staying at Miland Suites varies from $100 to $200 per night, depending on the room style and season.

Rigas Hotel

- Location: Hotel Rigas is located in Pollonia, a lovely town on Milos' northeastern shore. It is located near the beach and is surrounded by traditional tavernas and stores.

- Convenience to Major Attractions: The hotel is a short walk from Pollonia Beach and is close to other attractions such as Papafragas Beach and the Folklore and Maritime Museum. Plaka, a lovely town, is just a short drive away.

- Unique Features and Services: Hotel Rigas has spacious rooms and suites with contemporary facilities. Some rooms feature balconies or terraces with sea or garden views. The hotel has a pool, a restaurant providing Greek and foreign cuisine, and a comfortable lounge area.

- staying Costs: The projected cost of staying at Hotel Rigas varies from $100 to $200 per night, depending on the room type and season.

Aeolis Hotel

- Location: The Aeolis Hotel is in the town of Adamas and provides a handy base for touring Milos. It is near to the town center and within walking distance of Adamas' major attractions.

- Proximity to Major Attractions: The hotel is close to Adamas Beach and the vibrant seafront, which offers a variety of eating choices and stores. It's also close to major sights like Sarakiniko Beach and the Catacombs of Milos.

- Unique Features and Services: The Aeolis Hotel offers spacious rooms and suites with contemporary conveniences. Some rooms include balconies or terraces with views of the garden or the sea. The hotel has a pool, a restaurant that serves Greek and Mediterranean cuisine, and a bar.

- staying Costs: The projected cost of staying at Aeolis Hotel varies from $100 to $200 per night, depending on the room type and season.

Guesthouses:
Guesthouse Galini

- Location: Galini Guesthouse is in Plaka village, with panoramic views of the Aegean Sea and neighboring surroundings. It is located in a quiet neighborhood and offers a pleasant refuge.

- Walking Distance to Major Attractions: The guesthouse is within walking distance of Plaka's picturesque streets, traditional stores, and local tavernas. It is also near to the Catacombs of Milos, the Ancient Theater, and the Church of Panagia Korfiatissa.

- Unique Features and Services: Galini Guesthouse provides comfortable rooms decorated in classic Cycladic style. Private balconies or patios with views of the sea or the village are available in certain rooms. The guesthouse has a common sitting room, a garden, and free Wi-Fi.

- staying Costs: The projected cost of staying at Galini Guesthouse varies from $50 to $100 per night, depending on the room type and season.

Lithos Guesthouse
- Location: Lithos Guesthouse is located in the hamlet of Tripiti and provides a traditional and genuine Milos experience. It is close to Tripiti's main center and has a wonderful ambience.

- Proximity to Major Attractions: The Catacombs of Milos and the ancient town of Klima are both within walking distance of the guesthouse. It is also close to other sights like as Plaka, Sarakiniko Beach, and the Church of Agios Nikolaos.

- Unique Features and Services: Lithos Guesthouse offers comfortable rooms with classic stone walls and wooden furniture. Some accommodations have views of the Aegean Sea or the hamlet. The guesthouse has a common balcony, a shared kitchenette, and free Wi-Fi.

- staying Costs: Depending on the room type and season, the estimated cost of staying at Lithos Guesthouse varies from $50 to $100 per night.

Eiriana Luxury Suites

- Location: Eiriana Luxury Suites is situated in the Pollonia hamlet, providing a magnificent and serene location near the beach. It is close to the village's facilities as well as Milos' lovely shoreline.

- Proximity to Major Attractions: Pollonia Beach and the village's restaurants, cafés, and stores are all within walking distance of the suites. Popular neighboring sites include Papafragas Beach and the Folklore and Maritime Museum.

- Additional conveniences and Services: Eiriana Luxury Suites provides attractively built suites with contemporary conveniences and private balconies or patios. Some suites have views of the sea or direct access to the public pool. The rooms have a spa bath or a private outdoor hot tub, and concierge services are available.

- staying Estimate: The expected cost of staying at Eiriana Luxury Suites varies from $150 to $300 per night, depending on the room style and season.

Apartments and Studios
De Milo

- Location: En Milo is located in the hamlet of Adamas, close to the harbor and the town center. It is conveniently located near stores, restaurants, and the major attractions of Adamas.

- Proximity to Major Attractions: Adamas Beach, the promenade, and the ferry port are all within walking distance of the apartments. They are also close to sights like as Sarakiniko Beach and the Milos Catacombs.

- Unique Features and Services: En Milo offers pleasant flats and studios with fully equipped kitchens or kitchenettes where visitors may cook their own meals. Private balconies or patios are available in certain units. The hotel has free parking as well as free Wi-Fi.

- housing Costs: The projected cost of housing at En Milo varies from $70 to $150 per night, depending on apartment or studio size and season.

Semiramis Apartments

- Location: Semiramis Apartments is situated in Pollonia hamlet, giving a calm location near the beach. Pollonia's restaurants, cafés, and stores are all within walking distance.

- Convenience to Major Attractions: The flats are adjacent to Pollonia Beach and provide easy access to other attractions such as Papafragas Beach and the Folklore and Maritime Museum. Plaka, a lovely town, is just a short drive away.

Semiramis Apartments provides large and well-equipped apartments with separate bedrooms, living spaces, and kitchenettes. Private balconies or patios with sea views are available in certain units. The hotel has a swimming pool, a sun deck, and complimentary Wi-Fi.

- housing Costs: The projected cost of housing at Semiramis Apartments varies from $80 to $160 per night, depending on unit size and season.

Notos Villa

- Location: Villa Notos is located in the hamlet of Adamas, close to the town center and the harbor. It is close to stores, restaurants, and public transit.

- Proximity to Major Attractions: Adamas Beach, the promenade, and the town's major attractions are all within walking distance of the villa. It's also close to major attractions like Sarakiniko Beach and the Milos Catacombs.

- Unique Features and Services: Villa Notos provides large, fully furnished apartments and studios with contemporary conveniences. Private balconies or patios are available in certain units. The property has a lawn, BBQ grills, and free Wi-Fi.

- housing Costs: The projected cost of housing at Villa Notos varies from $80 to $150 per night, depending on apartment or studio size and season.

Budget accommodations
Pensiones and guesthouses
Suites Kapetan Tasos:

- Location: Kapetan Tasos Suites is situated in the town of Pollonia, close to the beach and the village center. It is close to Pollonia's restaurants, shopping, and sights.

- Proximity to Important sights: Pollonia Beach is within walking distance of the guesthouse, as are other famous sights like as Papafragas Beach and the Folklore and Maritime Museum.

- Unique Features and Services: Kapetan Tasos Suites provides pleasant and reasonably priced suites with basic facilities. Private balconies or patios are available in certain suites. The guesthouse offers free Wi-Fi and may help you arrange vehicle rentals or boat cruises.

- staying Estimate: The expected cost of staying at Kapetan Tasos Suites varies from $50 to $100 per night, depending on the room style and season.

Hotel Eleni

- Location: The Hotel Eleni is located in the hamlet of Adamas, close to the town center and the harbor. It is close to stores, restaurants, and public transit.

- Proximity to Major Attractions: Adamas Beach, the promenade, and the town's major attractions are all within walking distance of the hotel. It's also close to major attractions like Sarakiniko Beach and the Milos Catacombs.

- Unique Features and Services: Hotel Eleni provides affordable accommodations with minimal facilities. Balconies and patios are available in certain rooms. The hotel offers free Wi-Fi and can help you arrange car rentals or day excursions.

- staying Costs: The projected cost of staying at Hotel Eleni varies from $40 to $80 per night, depending on the room type and season.

George's Spot

- Location: George's Place is situated in the Pollonia village, close to the beach and the area's facilities. It is convenient to restaurants, cafés, and stores.

- Proximity to Important sights: Pollonia Beach is within walking distance of the guesthouse, as are sights like as Papafragas Beach and the Folklore and Maritime Museum.

- Unique Features and Services: George's Place provides inexpensive rooms and apartments with minimal facilities. Some lodgings feature balconies or patios. The guesthouse offers free Wi-Fi and may help you arrange transportation or island trips.

- staying Estimate: The expected cost of staying at George's Place varies from $30 to $60 per night, depending on the room or studio type and season.

Camping
Camping Achivadolimni

- Location: Achivadolimni Camping is near Achivadolimni Beach and provides a picturesque setting surrounded by nature. It is situated on Milos' southern shore, about 7 kilometers from Adamas.

- Proximity to Major Attractions: The camping area is adjacent to Achivadolimni Beach, where you may swim and participate in water sports. It is also close to other sights like as Sarakiniko Beach and the Milos Catacombs.

- Special Features and Services: Achivadolimni Camping has tent, camper, and caravan sites. Toilets, baths, a restaurant, and a mini-market are among the amenities. The camping area has immediate beach access and provides a peaceful and cost-effective lodging choice.

- Lodging Estimate: The anticipated cost of camping at Achivadolimni Camping varies from $10 to $20 per night, depending on the camping choice and season.

Glaronissi Camping

- Location: Glaronissi Camping is situated near the settlement of Provatas on Milos' northeastern shore. It is located in a scenic region surrounded by nature and provides a peaceful camping experience.

- Proximity to Major Attractions: The camping area is adjacent to Provatas Beach, where you may swim and relax. It is also close to other sights such as Tsigrado Beach and the Milos Catacombs.

- Special Features and Services: Glaronissi Camping has tent, camper, and caravan sites. The campground has basic amenities such as toilets, showers, and a mini-market. It is a cost-effective solution for individuals looking for a calm camping experience.

- Lodging Estimate: The anticipated cost of camping at Glaronissi Camping varies from $10 to $20 per night, depending on the camping choice and season.

Korfos Camping

- Location: Korfos Camping is located in the hamlet of Korfos, on the shore of Milos in the northeastern portion of the island. It offers convenient access to the beach as well as a tranquil setting for camping.

- Proximity to Major Attractions: The camping site is near Korfos Beach, where you may swim and sunbathe. It is also close to sights such as Sarakiniko Beach and the Catacombs of Milos.

- Special Features and Services: Korfos Camping provides tent and camper spaces. Toilets, showers, and a small café are available. For nature enthusiasts, the camping site offers a relaxed ambiance and an economical choice.

- Lodging Costs: The anticipated cost of camping in Korfos Camping varies from $10 to $20 per night, depending on the camping choice and season.

Please keep in mind that the fees listed above are estimates and may vary depending on variables such as the camping choice, season, and availability. For accurate price information, verify the particular rates and availability with the lodgings directly. Furthermore, camping locations may have special laws and restrictions, so it's best to enquire about any required permits or guidelines before arranging your camping vacation.

CHAPTER THREE
Exploring Major Cities
Plaka

Plaka, Milos' enchanting capital, is nestled on a mountaintop overlooking the brilliant Aegean Sea. With its small winding lanes and lovely whitewashed cottages, this historic town emanates a real Cycladic ambiance. Exploring Plaka enables tourists to go back in time, learn about the island's rich history, and take in the spectacular panoramic views that span the island and beyond.

Milos Archaeological Museum

The Milos Archaeological Museum, located in the center of Plaka, is a testimony to the island's rich historical past. The museum, housed in an attractive neoclassical edifice, displays a large collection of relics spanning thousands of years of human civilization on Milos.

The amazing exhibit of sculptures, ceramics, and statues that line the museum's hallways captures your attention the moment you walk in. The exhibitions give a window into the island's historic civilizations, providing insight into the lives, beliefs, and creative manifestations of the people who formerly lived here.

The Venus de Milo is one of the museum's most famous and acclaimed displays. This well-known marble statue, originating from the Hellenistic era, is a work of ancient Greek art. For generations, tourists have been captivated by its beautiful shape and mysterious countenance. Seeing the Venus de Milo in person is an unforgettable experience, as you marvel at the creativity and skill that went into making this legendary piece of art.

Aside from the Venus de Milo, the museum has a broad collection of objects that provide light on various times in Milos' history. Vases and figures made of intricately designed ceramics give insight into the island's creative heritage and everyday life. Elaborate sculptures, some portraying legendary characters and others local deities, provide insight into the ancient Milians' religious beliefs.

The Milos Ancient Museum not only displays these extraordinary items but also gives contextual information and interpretation, enabling visitors to have a better knowledge of the island's ancient legacy. Informative signs and well-designed exhibitions lead you through the galleries, uncovering the tales and importance of each object.

Visiting Milos' Archaeological Museum is like traveling back in time and immersing yourself in the island's ancient history. It provides a once-in-a-lifetime chance to appreciate Milos' creative accomplishments and cultural richness, as well as get a better knowledge of the historical events and influences that molded the island's identity.

As you leave the museum, you'll have a renewed respect for the ancient civilizations that once flourished on Milos, as well as a stronger connection to the island's unique past. The Milos Archaeological Museum is a must-see for anybody interested in the cultural history and archaeological treasures of this picturesque Greek island.

Panagia Korfiatissa Church

The Panagia Korfiatissa Church, perched magnificently above Plaka's highest point, is both an architectural marvel and a vital religious institution. This lovely Orthodox church, dedicated to the Virgin Mary, dates from the 17th century. Its beautiful white exterior is capped with a remarkable blue dome and graceful bell tower. When you go inside, you'll be enveloped by a peaceful ambiance produced by magnificent paintings, holy symbols, and shimmering candles. Panoramic views of the island's sceneries extend from the church's courtyard, providing a spectacular perspective that includes the turquoise sea, undulating hills, and surrounding islands.

Kastro of Plaka (Castle)

The Kastro of Plaka is a relic of Milos' medieval history and a fascinating historic landmark inside the hamlet. This fortified sector, which dates back to the 13th century, played an important role in safeguarding the island from pirate invasions. You'll feel transported to another age as you walk through its small cobblestone streets and stone archways. Discover secret chapels, classic Cycladic dwellings, and castle wall fragments that provide insight into the island's architectural legacy. Ascending to the Kastro's highest point provides tourists with breathtaking panoramic views of the mountainous coastline, which is studded with lovely fishing towns and isolated beaches.

Exploring Plaka's picturesque alleyways provides an enthralling combination of culture, history, and natural beauty. The Milos Archaeological Museum reveals the island's ancient history, while the Panagia Korfiatissa Church and Kastro provide light on its religious and medieval histories, respectively. Plaka encompasses the spirit of Milos and allows tourists to immerse themselves in its compelling beauty and timeless attraction, from the small alleys to the stunning vistas.

Adamas

Adamas, on Milos' northern shore, is a lively port town that serves as the island's major entrance point. Its dynamic atmosphere, scenic waterfront, and diverse assortment of activities make it a popular tourist destination. Adamas provides a beautiful combination of nautical charm and cultural legacy, from touring the picturesque harbor to visiting cultural treasures.

Adamas Port

The scenic port of Adamas serves as a center of activity and an entrance to the island. A vibrant sight of fishing boats, yachts, and traditional tavernas awaits you as you wander along the waterfront promenade. The port area is dotted with cafés, restaurants, and stores, making it an ideal place to unwind and take in the colorful atmosphere.

The port of Adamas is more than simply a destination for leisurely strolls; it also provides a variety of amenities to guests. From here, you may board ferries to neighboring Greek islands or go on boat cruises to explore Milos' beautiful coastline and secret bays. The port also serves as a departure point for organized excursions to local sights such as the well-known Kleftiko caverns and the volcanic landscapes of Sarakiniko Beach.

Milos Mining Museum
The Milos Mining Museum, located near the harbor, offers an intriguing look into the island's mining past. Milos has a long history of mining, mainly for minerals including obsidian, sulfur, and kaolin. The museum highlights the island's diverse geological history as well as the influence of mining on its growth.

The museum has a variety of mining equipment, machinery, and interactive exhibits that demonstrate the processes involved in mineral extraction and processing. Exhibits illustrate the historical importance of mining on Milos, as well as its impact on the local economy and culture. Visitors may learn about the geological formations of the island, the many minerals found on Milos, and the methods used by miners throughout the years.

The Church of the Holy Trinity
The Church of the Holy Trinity is a significant landmark in Adamas, perched on a hill overlooking the town. This lovely whitewashed church, with its characteristic blue dome and bell tower, is a place of worship for the local community. As you approach the church,

you'll see a peaceful courtyard filled with brilliant flowers and shaded by old olive trees.

Step inside to discover a tranquil haven filled with exquisite Byzantine-inspired paintings, holy symbols, and intricate woodwork. The interior oozes peace and respect, allowing visitors to rest and think. The chapel also provides spectacular panoramic views of Adamas and the surrounding shoreline, making it an ideal setting for reflection and photography.

Exploring Adamas provides tourists with the opportunity to enjoy the vivid atmosphere of a classic Greek waterfront town. The port is a hive of activity, providing a range of services and chances for exploration. The Milos Mining Museum gives a unique insight into the island's geological past and mining traditions, while the Church of the Holy Trinity provides a tranquil refuge with panoramic views of the town. Adamas is a must-see site that highlights Milos' unique attractions and cultural treasures.

Pollonia

Pollonia, located on Milos' northeast coast, is a quiet fishing hamlet with a laid-back character and breathtaking beauty. Pollonia provides a tranquil respite from the busy throng, with its beautiful beaches, traditional tavernas, and genuine hospitality, making it an ideal place for relaxation and renewal.

When you arrive at Pollonia, you'll notice the gorgeous landscape right away. The sandy beaches, crystal-clear oceans, and craggy shoreline offer a magnificent setting that encourages you to relax and enjoy nature's splendor. The hamlet itself is a picturesque collection of whitewashed homes, tiny alleyways, and bright bougainvillea, giving it a real Cycladic feel.

Milos Folklore Museum

The Milos Folklore Museum, located in the center of Pollonia, offers a unique glimpse into the island's traditional way of life.

The museum, housed in a lovely stone edifice, displays a variety of antiques and exhibits that represent Milos' rich cultural legacy.

The museum has a number of exhibits that showcase the island's folklore, customs, and traditions. The museum provides a complete picture of the local culture, ranging from traditional costumes and musical instruments to household objects and handicrafts. Each exhibit comes with an explanatory explanation that provides context and historical context.

The traditional living environment replicated inside the walls of the Folklore Museum is one of its most prominent features. You may go back in time and see how Milos inhabitants lived in the past. The traditional furniture, household objects, and décor provide insight into the island's residents' everyday life.

The museum also conducts cultural events and exhibits that include local artists and craftspeople, which enhances the tourist experience. These events provide a chance to interact with the island's lively artistic community and obtain a better understanding of Milos' creative past.

Visiting the Milos Folklore Museum in Pollonia gives you a better insight of the island's cultural origins and customs. It enables you to comprehend the rituals and folklore that have created Milos' identity throughout the years. The museum acts as a time capsule, providing insight into the lives and customs of the island's population.

Beyond the museum, Pollonia itself provides a tranquil setting for rest and exploration. Spend your days relaxing on the sandy beaches, eating delicious seafood at waterfront tavernas, or taking boat cruises to adjacent islands and secret coves. Pollonia is a pleasant and peaceful location that encapsulates Milos' natural beauty and cultural legacy.

Top Attractions and Activities

Sarakiniko Beach

Sarakiniko Beach, located on Milos' northern shore, is a one-of-a-kind and enchanting natural marvel that captivates tourists with its unearthly beauty. This breathtaking beach is known for its lunar-like terrain, which consists of brilliant white volcanic rock formations carved by wind and waves over millions of years.

A stunning vista will welcome you as you approach Sarakiniko Beach. The whole shoreline is covered with smooth, white volcanic rocks that seem like they belong on the moon. The juxtaposition of the gleaming white rocks and the deep blue water produces a weird and ethereal ambiance unlike anything you've ever seen.

The rock formations at Sarakiniko Beach are the product of volcanic activity that happened thousands of years ago in the region. Over time, the volcanic ash and lava flow consolidated and eroded, forming fascinating forms and patterns that excite photographers and wildlife lovers. There are unique structures such as arches, caverns, and hollows that invite you to explore and marvel at nature's marvels.

The beach itself is a cluster of smooth rocks that flow gently into the blue waters of the Aegean Sea, rather than a traditional sandy beach. Although not perfect for sunbathing, Sarakiniko Beach's distinctive scenery provides enough options for exploration and relaxation.

Swimming in the crystal-clear waters is one of the attractions of a visit to Sarakiniko Beach. The small, tranquil water is ideal for a refreshing swim, and the surrounding rocks create natural platforms for sunbathing and taking in the breathtaking views. Snorkelers will be amazed by the underwater environment, which is alive with marine life and provides a wonderful experience of exploring the vivid Mediterranean sea.

It's important to note that, owing to the absence of natural cover, you should carry sunscreen, hats, and umbrellas to protect yourself from the hot Greek heat. It is also advisable to wear proper footwear, such as water shoes, while walking on the smooth rocks.

Sarakiniko Beach is more than simply a day trip. It has a particular fascination in the evenings, when the setting sun creates a warm light on the white rocks, creating a lovely ambiance. The sunset from Sarakiniko Beach is a unique experience that will leave you in awe of Milos' natural beauty.

Remember to practice responsible tourism and preserve the environment while visiting Sarakiniko Beach. By avoiding removing or destroying any rocks or flora, you may help to conserve this unique terrain.

Sarakiniko Beach is a must-see site on the island of Milos. Its remarkable lunar-like scenery, crystal-clear seas, and distinctive geological formations make it a nature lover's, photographer's, and beachgoer's heaven. Immerse yourself in Sarakiniko Beach's ethereal beauty and let its wonderful ambiance carry you to another dimension.

Kleftiko

Kleftiko is a hidden treasure located along Milos' southern shore. Kleftiko, known for its stunning sea caverns, provides an unforgettable experience that will leave you in awe of the island's natural beauty.

You may join a boat trip or charter a private boat from Adamas or Pollonia to go to Kleftiko. As you approach the location, you will be met by towering cliffs and rocky outcrops rising from the brilliant blue seas. These cliffs feature a series of spectacular sea caves that have been carved out through time by the water's unrelenting strength.

The sea caves in Kleftiko are breathtaking. They create a bizarre and magical ambiance with their towering arches, complex structures, and vivid hues. By boat, you may explore the caverns' depths and watch the interplay of light and shadows as sunlight streams through the entrances, revealing the crystal-clear waters beneath.

The caverns are not only physically magnificent, but also a playground for adventure seekers. Snorkeling and diving at Kleftiko's waters show a thriving underwater environment rich with marine life. Swim with colorful fish, look out for inquisitive octopuses, and see the vivid corals that flourish in this protected marine habitat.

You'll be able to dock your boat and go ashore on tiny rocky islands while exploring Kleftiko. These islands provide isolated areas for sunbathing, picnics, and admiring the scenery. The crystal-clear waters encourage you to swim or just lay on the surface, immersing yourself in the serenity of this natural paradise.

It is crucial to note that the sea caves of Kleftiko are best approached by boat, since the topography and currents make land access problematic. Boat trips depart often from Milos, and skilled local guides may take you on a wonderful voyage while telling tales and legends about Kleftiko.

When visiting Kleftiko, it is essential to protect the natural environment and adhere to sustainable tourism practices. Avoid leaving any rubbish behind and keep the precious marine ecology in mind. It's also a good idea to pack sunscreen, snorkeling equipment, and proper footwear for exploring the caverns and rough terrain.

Kleftiko is a real Milos jewel, delivering a one-of-a-kind and awe-inspiring experience. A mesmerizing ambiance is created by the mix of beautiful sea caves, crystal-clear seas, and breathtaking rock formations. Immerse yourself in the splendor of Kleftiko and let the natural wonder's enchantment captivate you.

Papafragas Beach

Papafragas Beach, located on Milos' northeastern shore, is a hidden treasure just waiting to be found. This little, quiet beach, flanked by towering cliffs and turquoise waves, provides a one-of-a-kind and magical experience.

To get to Papafragas Beach, use a trail that weaves through the rocky environment and leads down to the sandy coastline. As you make your way down, you'll be met with stunning cliffs that envelop the shore, providing a natural amphitheater-like scene. The cliffs provide a feeling of isolation and privacy, making Papafragas Beach seem like your own little sanctuary.

The beach is quite tiny, with smooth golden sand and crystal-clear seas that encourage you to swim. The bay's peaceful and shallow conditions make it perfect for relaxing bathing and snorkeling, enabling you to explore the underwater world and meet colorful marine species.

One of Papafragas Beach's distinguishing characteristics is a tiny entrance on the cliffside that leads to a secret sea cave. Enter this magical tunnel to find a secret alcove where sunlight seeps through, producing a stunning glow on the blue waters below. It's a great place to soak in nature's splendor and snap amazing images.

Papafragas Beach has a quiet and serene ambiance due to its remote position. It's ideal for getting away from the throng and immersing yourself in the tranquillity of the surroundings. The lack of beach facilities and amenities adds to the beach's pristine and natural attractiveness.

It is critical to be prepared while visiting Papafragas Beach. There are no local restaurants or stores, so pack food, beverages, and any other necessities you may need for your stay. Furthermore, since there is little cover, it is advised to carry sun protection, such as sunscreen, hats, and umbrellas, to protect oneself from the sun's rays.

Papafragas Beach is a wonderful hidden treasure on Milos, giving a serene and gorgeous environment that will steal your heart. It's quiet setting, magnificent cliffs, and secret sea cave combine to provide an unforgettable and captivating experience. Take the time to discover this hidden gem and enjoy the beauty of Papafragas Beach.

Plathiena Beach

Plathiena Beach, located on Milos' southern shore, is a gorgeous paradise famed for its crystal clear waves and unspoiled beauty. This lovely beach provides a serene respite and is ideal for relaxing and unwinding.

As you approach Plathiena Beach, you'll see a beautiful expanse of golden sand that gradually dips into the Aegean Sea's blue seas. The beach is distinguished by its smooth and fine sand, which makes it ideal for sunbathing and leisurely strolls along the coastline.

Plathiena Beach is known for its unusually pure and crystalline seas. The stunning tones of blue entice you to enjoy a refreshing plunge. The peaceful and serene bay provides a safe swimming environment for both adults and children. The underwater world will also excite snorkelers, as the clean waters provide good vision and the chance to explore the marine fauna that inhabits the region.

Plathiena Beach is encircled by stunning cliffs that provide peace and serenity. These natural rocks produce a protected cove that protects the beach from severe winds and creates a tranquil and serene ambiance. It's the ideal location to get away from it all, relax on the soft sand, and listen to the calm lapping of the waves.

While Plathiena Beach provides a tranquil setting, it also offers some essential conveniences to improve your beach experience. Sun loungers and umbrellas may be rented, enabling you to rest in comfort and shade. A beach bar is also available where you may quench your thirst or enjoy some light snacks.

It's worth noting that Plathiena Beach may become fairly crowded during the peak summer months, so go there early to get a nice place. Furthermore, the absence of natural shade necessitates the use of sun protection, such as sunscreen, hats, and umbrellas, to protect oneself from the sun's rays.

Plathiena Beach is a genuine paradise for anyone looking for crystal clear seas and a relaxing beach experience. Its breathtaking scenery, tranquil waves, and golden sand combine to create a haven of leisure and natural magnificence. Immerse yourself in the tranquillity of Plathiena Beach and let the crystal clear seas wash away your concerns as you enjoy Milos' natural beauty.

Milos Catacombs

The Milos Catacombs are a magnificent archaeological site that provides an intriguing peek into the island's past history. These catacombs, located just outside the hamlet of Tripiti, are one of Greece's greatest early Christian burial places and have important historical and cultural significance.

When you enter the catacombs, you'll be transported back in time and immersed in a subterranean maze of twisting hallways and rooms. In the first century AD, these catacombs were excavated out of soft volcanic rock and used as a burial ground for early Christians for many decades.

The catacombs are a network of intricately interwoven tiny corridors, chambers, and graves. The catacombs' exceptional design and workmanship are breathtaking, demonstrating the inventiveness and ability of Milos' ancient inhabitants. While walking through these old passageways, you will be able to view several burial niches and rooms that were utilized for diverse reasons.

Exploring the Milos Catacombs is a one-of-a-kind and informative experience. It provides visitors with an insight into the early Christian period, letting them comprehend burial traditions and religious rituals of the time. You'll come across well-preserved paintings and inscriptions along the path that gives insight into the lives of people who were put to rest here.

Because the catacombs are protected and conserved, seeing them needs a guided tour. The subterranean pathways will be conducted by knowledgeable interpreters who will provide historical and cultural facts about the catacombs and its importance. It's a good idea to verify the tour itinerary and availability ahead of time, particularly during high tourist season.

The Milos Catacombs are a location of profound veneration and respect. It is important to have a polite manner when visiting the catacombs, since they are religiously and historically significant. Because photography may be prohibited in some locations, it is best to adhere to the rules stated by the guides.

When visiting the Milos Catacombs, it's best to wear comfortable shoes since the subterranean pathways might be uneven and barely lighted. Bring a light jacket or sweater as well, since the temperature within the catacombs is usually colder than outside.

The Milos Catacombs offers an intriguing excursion into the island's history and a fuller appreciation of its rich cultural legacy. Exploring these subterranean passageways and seeing the preserved tombs and artworks is certainly a once-in-a-lifetime experience. Explore Milos' ancient history and uncover the mysteries buried beneath the Catacombs of Milos.

Ancient Theatre of Milos

The Ancient Theatre of Milos, perched on a hillside overlooking the picturesque town of Tripiti, is a testimony to the island's rich cultural legacy. This beautifully-preserved amphitheater provides a breathtaking background for theatrical performances and cultural activities, as well as a view into the ancient world.

The Ancient Theatre of Milos originates from the third century BC and was built by the ancient Greeks. The theater, which was carved into the natural slope of the hill, has outstanding acoustics and can seat a huge number of people. It was largely utilized for theatrical productions such as plays, comedies, and musical events, which brought the community together for amusement and cultural festivals.

The majesty of the old edifice will meet you as you enter the theater. The auditorium, a semicircular seating area, provides a commanding perspective of the stage, ensuring that every seat gets an excellent view of the events. The tiered stone seats provide a feeling of grandeur and recreate the mood of ancient Greek theatre.

The Ancient Theatre of Milos is an enthralling backdrop for a variety of cultural events and performances. The theater comes alive throughout the summer months with theatrical shows, concerts, and other cultural acts. You'll be taken back in time and absorbed in the bright energy of the performances as you sit beneath the open sky, surrounded by the ruins of old structures.

Aside from its historical and cultural value, the theater also provides spectacular views of the surrounding environment. From the top rows of the sitting area, you can take in the lovely Milos shoreline, the quaint town of Tripiti, and the glittering Aegean Sea. It's an excellent location for taking beautiful photos and admiring the island's natural splendor.

Visiting Milos' historic Theatre is a remarkable experience for history buffs, theater fans, and anybody looking for a deeper connection to the island's historic past. The venue is a short walk from Tripiti's hamlet, and there is no entry cost to attend the theater. However, it is best to double-check the operating hours and any booked activities ahead of time.

It is suggested that visitors wear comfortable shoes while visiting the Ancient Theatre of Milos, since there are stairs and uneven ground throughout the theater. Bring sun protection, such as hats and sunscreen, since there is minimal shade.

Visit the Ancient Theatre to immerse yourself in Milos' rich history and cultural tradition. Witness the historic structure's grandeur, take in the spectacular vistas, and be transported to a period when theater and the arts flourished in this charming corner of Greece.

Sailing and Boat Tours

Sailing or boat tours are one of the most popular and exciting activities in Milos. Milos is a haven for sea lovers and adventure enthusiasts, with its beautiful coastline, secluded coves, and spectacular rock formations.

Sailing and boat cruises are great ways to see the island from a different viewpoint and find its hidden jewels. There are several alternatives available to fit your tastes and interests, whether you are a seasoned sailor or a first-time explorer.

Many tour companies in Milos offer half-day or full-day sailing adventures that enable you to traverse the Aegean Sea while seeing some of the most beautiful places on the island. Depending on your desired style and party size, you may select between catamarans, sailing boats, or classic wooden boats.

A sailing excursion will allow you to see Milos' stunning coastline, which is lined with towering cliffs, hidden caves, and isolated beaches. The stunning sea caves of Kleftiko, famed for their distinctive rock formations and blue seas, are often the focus of these journeys. You may swim, snorkel, or just rest on the deck while admiring the breathtaking scenery that surrounds you.

Sailing cruises may include visits at other amazing beaches and attractions, such as Sarakiniko Beach, Firiplaka Beach, or the Papafragas Sea Cave, in addition to Kleftiko. The expert team aboard will augment your experience by providing insights into the geological formations, history, and local folklore linked with each place.

There are boat excursions that appeal to certain interests in addition to sailing trips. Some trips are centered on fishing, enabling you to try your hand at catching local fish while being guided by professional fisherman. Others provide sunset cruises where you may marvel at the spectacular hues of the sky as the sun sets below the horizon.

It is best to schedule a sailing or boat excursion in Milos in advance, particularly during the busy tourist season. Prices and trip lengths may vary based on the operator and the kind of tour you choose. To guarantee a pleasant and happy visit, learn about the services offered, such as snorkeling equipment, beverages, and meals.

A sailing or boat excursion in Milos promises to be a remarkable and thrilling experience, whether you're looking for adventure, leisure, or a mix of the two. Prepare to be charmed by the island's natural beauty, enjoy the invigorating sea wind, and to make amazing memories as you begin on a journey of discovery in the blue seas of the Aegean Sea.

Firiplaka Beach

Firiplaka Beach, located on Milos' southern shore, is a real paradise that combines natural beauty and solitude. The magnificent drive down the coastal road, with vistas of the turquoise sea and craggy rocks, will fascinate you as you make your way to the beach.

When you arrive to Firiplaka Beach, you'll see the golden sand that spreads for around 300 meters down the beach. The smooth, fine sand is ideal for reclining and sunbathing, so bring a beach blanket or hire a sunbed for extra relaxation. Even during high season, the beach is very vast, enabling people to find their own space and solitude.

Firiplaka Beach's tranquil and crystal-clear blue waves are welcoming and great for swimming. The moderate slope of the seabed makes it excellent for swimmers of all ages and abilities. You may cool down with a nice swim or just walk in the shallow waters, enjoying the calming feeling of the soft waves lapping at your feet.

Firiplaka Beach is distinguished by its spectacular cliffs, which give natural shelter and form a dramatic background. There are protected areas behind the cliffs where you may rest and enjoy the spectacular views of the Aegean Sea while avoiding the sun. It's the ideal place to read a book, enjoy a picnic, or just relax and take in the scenery.

Firiplaka Beach offers thrilling water sports activities for anyone looking for a little adventure. You may explore the neighboring coastline by renting paddleboards or kayaks and exploring secret coves, little caves, and quiet beaches. Snorkeling is also a popular pastime due to the abundance of marine life and gorgeous underwater scenery in the seas around Firiplaka Beach.

When it's time to refuel, there are beachside bars and cafés along Firiplaka Beach. These restaurants provide a variety of cuisines, ranging from fresh seafood to classic Greek specialities. You may experience the delicacies of the area while admiring the breathtaking views of the beach and water.

Firiplaka Beach is a popular location for both residents and visitors, so come early, particularly during peak season, to ensure a decent place on the beach. Showers and toilets are provided for the convenience of guests.

Overall, Firiplaka Beach on Milos Island is a piece of heaven, combining natural beauty, leisure, and adventure chances. Firiplaka Beach provides something for everyone, whether you're looking for sun and sand, water activities, or a peaceful place to rest.

Tsigrado Beach

Tsigrado Beach's charm resides in its raw and untouched nature. The lack of services and commercialization contributes to its allure, allowing visitors to completely immerse themselves in the natural surroundings. To make the most of your time at this quiet paradise, bring your own beach umbrella, towels, and a picnic lunch.

Tsigrado Beach's distinctive rock formations are one of its main attractions. The rocks that surround the beach include tiny gaps and little caverns that contribute to the mystery and exploration. Climbers and adventurers may explore these granite formations, uncovering secret nooks and crannies along the way.

Tsigrado Beach's tranquil, crystal-clear waters are ideal for swimming and snorkeling. Dive into the cool waters to uncover a thriving underwater world alive with marine life. Snorkeling equipment is required to truly experience the beauty under the surface.

Tsigrado Beach provides a feeling of tranquillity and seclusion that is difficult to get elsewhere due to its isolated position. It's great for people looking for a peaceful retreat and an opportunity to reconnect with nature. Because there are less people, you may rest, unwind, and listen to the calming sound of the waves breaking against the rocks.

The steep and narrow entrance route to Tsigrado Beach requires a certain degree of physical fitness and agility. It may not be ideal for those with limited mobility or tiny children. Wear proper footwear with adequate traction and proceed with care throughout the descent.

Visiting Tsigrado Beach is a once-in-a-lifetime opportunity. It provides a glimpse of unadulterated natural beauty as well as an opportunity to disengage from the rush and bustle of daily life. To maintain the pristine state of this hidden jewel, remember to respect the environment and leave no trace.

Because Tsigrado Beach is inaccessible by public transit, it is best to hire a vehicle or a scooter to go to this distant site. Plan your visit appropriately, since arriving early to get a parking place and escape the noon heat is recommended. Accept the challenge and immerse yourself in the tranquillity of Tsigrado Beach, a truly hidden gem on Milos Island.

Paliochori Beach

Paliochori Beach is also noted for its busy beach scene and energetic vibe. The beachside bars and cafés provide a lively atmosphere, particularly during the high summer months. While taking in the magnificent views of the Aegean Sea, you may have a meal or a refreshing drink.

The volcanic scenery is one of Paliochori Beach's features. The cliffs that surround the beach are stunningly colored, ranging from red and orange to yellow and white. This colourful show is the consequence of millions of years of volcanic activity that created the island. Exploring the cliffs and marveling at their distinct geological structures is an unforgettable experience.

The hot springs of Paliochori Beach are very appealing. The naturally heated water generates hot patches on the beach, creating a one-of-a-kind swimming experience. You may rest in a shallow hole dug in the sand while warm water envelops you, providing a natural thermal spa-like experience. It's a relaxing and calming experience that adds to Paliochori Beach's attractiveness.

The beach's position on Milos' southern shore offers for spectacular sunset views. The sky morphs into a painting of vivid colours as the sun starts to drop over the horizon, spreading a golden light over the sea and the surrounding rocks. It's a spectacular sight that shouldn't be missed, and Paliochori Beach is an excellent vantage point to watch it.

Paliochori Beach is a popular site for both residents and tourists, thus arriving early is recommended, particularly during the high summer season. The beach has a range of facilities for hire, including beach loungers, umbrellas, and water sports equipment. The adjacent taverns provide a variety of delectable Greek cuisine, such as fresh fish, classic mezze, and regional delicacies.

Paliochori Beach provides a well-rounded experience that appeals to diverse desires, whether you're looking for leisure, natural beauty, or a busy beach scene. It's a beach where you can soak up the rays, cool down in the Aegean Sea, explore the unique volcanic environment, and enjoy the lively atmosphere. Include Paliochori Beach on your Milos Island itinerary for a memorable beach experience.

Milos Volcanic Landscape

Milos Island is famous for its distinctive and intriguing volcanic terrain, which bears witness to the island's turbulent geological past. The geology of the island is the consequence of millions of years of severe volcanic activity. Milos was fashioned into the beautiful island it is today by volcanic eruptions and subsequent geological processes.

Milos' volcanic terrain is distinguished by its various rock formations, steep cliffs, and brilliant hues. The island is home to a diverse range of volcanic materials, including pumice, obsidian, and tuff. The textures and hues of these rocks vary from porous and lightweight pumice to shiny and black obsidian.

Milos' caldera is one of the island's most recognizable geological features. The Milos Caldera, the island's central bay, is the remains of a volcanic crater produced after a violent eruption. The caldera is encircled by magnificent cliffs, which provide a stunning background for the island's coastal districts.

Milos' volcanic activity has also resulted in several unusual geological structures. Sarakiniko Beach, for example, has a lunar-like environment sculpted by wind and sea erosion with its white volcanic rocks. The formations are reminiscent of a moonscape, with smooth curves, hollows, and gaps creating a bizarre and otherworldly environment.

Sulphur Mines and Hot Springs

Milos Island is well-known for its natural hot springs, which provide guests a healing and revitalizing experience. Geothermal activity causes warm water from deep inside the Earth's crust to rise to the surface, resulting in these hot springs. The warm waters are filled with minerals like as sulfur, magnesium, and calcium, which are recognized for their therapeutic capabilities and health benefits.

Paliochori Beach, situated on Milos Island's southern shore, is one of the most prominent destinations for hot springs. Thermal springs provide pockets of warm water along the coastline, providing a one-of-a-kind bathing experience. The water temperature fluctuates, and you may choose to relax in the soothing warmth while you soak in the mineral-rich waters. The hot springs at Paliochori Beach are an ideal place to rest and unwind while also taking in the stunning scenery of the beach.

Agia Kyriaki Beach is another neighboring area where you may enjoy hot springs. Underground hot springs combine with saltwater to provide a pleasant and relaxing swimming environment. You'll feel the soothing effects of the minerals on your skin as you dive into the waters, delivering a tranquil and renewing experience.

Milos Island is also noted for its ancient sulphur mines, in addition to its hot springs. Sulphur, a yellow mineral with a wide range of industrial uses, was formerly a valuable natural resource on the island. In the past, sulphur mining was important to the island's economy and growth. While the mines are no longer in use, you may still visit the ruins and learn about the island's mining history. The abandoned mines and buildings serve as a reminder of the island's industrial history, providing insight into the life of the miners who worked there.

Visiting Milos Island's hot springs and sulphur mines gives a unique viewpoint on the island's geothermal activity and historical importance. Whether you want to soak in the healing waters of the hot springs or learn about the island's mining history, you'll be immersed in the island's natural and cultural marvels.

Sea Caves and Rock Formations

Milos Island's Sea caves and rock formations are testaments to the island's natural marvels and give tourists with a unique and magical experience.

Kleftiko is a well-known sea cave complex on Milos Island. Kleftiko, located on the southwest coast, is a collection of spectacular caverns molded by the unrelenting power of the sea over thousands of years. These caverns can only be reached by boat, adding to the thrill of the expedition. As you approach Kleftiko, you'll be met by towering white cliffs rising from the blue ocean, providing a breathtaking background. The caverns themselves provide a wonderful backdrop, complete with secret coves, arches, and tunnels just waiting to be explored. Inside the caverns, you'll get a close look at the magnificent rock formations, marveling at their unique patterns and textures. The crystal-clear seas around Kleftiko are ideal for swimming and snorkeling, letting you to experience the natural marvel even more.

The "Syrmata" near the picturesque fishing town of Klima is another famous rock feature on Milos Island. These bright and attractive boathouses are carved into the cliffs, providing a lively and one-of-a-kind scene. Historically, local fishermen utilized the Syrmata to store their boats and fishing equipment. They have been converted into attractive hotels, allowing guests to stay in these traditional and culturally valuable buildings. The Syrmata provide a look into the island's nautical history and serve as a reminder of the local community's intimate interaction with the water.

Exploring Milos Island's sea caves and rock formations is an excursion that immerses you in the island's natural beauty and geological wonders. Whether you're traveling through the caverns of Kleftiko, enjoying the exquisite rock formations, or gazing at the bright Syrmata in Klima, the island's coastline attractions will fascinate you. These natural structures are a tribute to nature's force and craftsmanship, providing tourists with long-lasting impressions of Milos' spectacular scenery. Milos Island's Sea caves and rock formations are testaments to the island's natural marvels and give tourists with a unique and magical experience.

Kleftiko is a well-known sea cave complex on Milos Island. Kleftiko, located on the southwest coast, is a collection of spectacular caverns molded by the unrelenting power of the sea over thousands of years. These caverns can only be reached by boat, adding to the thrill of the expedition. As you approach Kleftiko, you'll be met by towering white cliffs rising from the blue ocean, providing a breathtaking background. The caverns themselves provide a wonderful backdrop, complete with secret coves, arches, and tunnels just waiting to be explored. Inside the caverns, you'll get a close look at the magnificent rock formations, marveling at their unique patterns and textures. The crystal-clear seas around Kleftiko are ideal for swimming and snorkeling, letting you experience the natural marvel even more.

The "Syrmata" near the picturesque fishing town of Klima is another famous rock feature on Milos Island. These bright and attractive boathouses are carved into the cliffs, providing a lively and one-of-a-kind scene. Historically, local fishermen utilized the Syrmata to store their boats and fishing equipment. They have been converted into attractive hotels, allowing guests to stay in these traditional and culturally valuable buildings. The Syrmata provide a look into the island's nautical history and serve as a reminder of the local community's intimate interaction with the water.

Exploring Milos Island's Sea caves and rock formations is an excursion that immerses you in the island's natural beauty and geological wonders. Whether you're traveling through the caverns of Kleftiko, enjoying the exquisite rock formations, or gazing at the bright Syrmata in Klima, the island's coastline attractions will fascinate you. These natural structures are a tribute to nature's force and craftsmanship, providing tourists with long-lasting impressions of Milos' spectacular scenery.

Milos Island's volcanic terrain, hot springs, and distinctive rock formations provide a compelling combination of natural beauty and geological mysteries. Visitors may admire the environment by exploring these features.

The island's complex geological history and the enormous forces that have sculpted its spectacular scenery. Milos has a geological tapestry that will leave you in wonder of nature's creative force, from lunar-like beaches to secret sea caverns.

CHAPTER FOUR
Local Cuisine and Dining

When it comes to eating on Milos Island, you can expect to sample a variety of classic Greek cuisine that highlights the island's rich culinary history. Here are some typical Greek foods that you should taste when in Greece.

Greek Dishes
Moussaka

Moussaka is a layered dish comprised of eggplant, ground meat (often beef or lamb), and a creamy béchamel sauce. Typically, the eggplant is sliced and roasted before being covered with meat sauce and topped with béchamel. After that, it is cooked till golden and served hot. The mix of tastes and textures results in a substantial and pleasant meal known as Greek comfort cuisine.

Souvlaki

Souvlaki is a famous Greek street snack consisting of skewered and grilled meat, usually pig or chicken. Before grilling, the meat is marinated in olive oil, lemon juice, and herbs. Souvlaki is traditionally served with pita bread, tzatziki sauce (made with yogurt, cucumber, garlic, and dill), and a variety of garnishes including tomatoes, onions, and lettuce. It's a tasty and easy alternative for a fast and tasty supper.

Horiatiki

Horiatiki, or Greek salad, is a light and colorful meal prepared with fresh tomatoes, cucumbers, red onions, Kalamata olives, and feta cheese. Typically, the salad is seasoned with olive oil, lemon juice, and dried oregano. It's a light and healthful dish that emphasizes the vivid taste of Mediterranean ingredients.

Spanakopita

Spanakopita is A delicious pastry stuffed with spinach, feta cheese, onions, and herbs. The filling is cooked between layers of flaky phyllo pastry until brown and crunchy. Spanakopita is a popular appetizer or snack with a delectable blend of tastes and textures.

Dolmades

Dolmades are stuffed grape leaves filled with rice, seasonings, and sometimes minced meat. Rolling the grape leaves around the filling creates bite-sized pieces. Dolmades may be eaten hot or cold and are often paired with tzatziki sauce. They're a tasty and filling appetizer that highlights the use of fragrant herbs in Greek cooking.

Seafood Delight

1. Fresh Grilled Fish: Milos Island has an abundance of fresh seafood, and grilled fish is one of the greatest ways to enjoy it. Sea bream, sea bass, red mullet, and sardines are popular roasted over an open flame. To accentuate the natural qualities of the fish, it is frequently seasoned with herbs, olive oil, and lemon. Grilled fish is a simple but tasty alternative that highlights the freshness and quality of the seafood.

2. Octopus: Octopus is a famous Greek seafood dish, and Milos Island is no exception. Grilled octopus is a popular way of preparation, in which the octopus is marinated in olive oil, lemon juice, garlic, and herbs before being grilled over a flame. As a consequence, the octopus is soft and tasty, with a little scorched skin. It is often accompanied with a drizzle of olive oil, a squeeze of fresh lemon juice, and a sprinkle of herbs.

3. Psarosoupa, or fish soup, is a classic Greek meal cooked with various fish, vegetables, herbs, and olive oil. Typically, the fish is cooked in a delicious broth with vegetables such as onions, tomatoes, carrots, and celery. Herbs like as parsley, dill, and bay leaves are often used to season the soup. Psarosoupa is a healthy and pleasant meal that highlights the tastes of the sea.

4. Astakos (Lobster): For a genuinely decadent seafood experience, try Astakos.

Try the astakos, often known as lobster. Milos Island is well-known for its excellent lobster, which may be served in a variety of ways. Popular preparations include grilled lobster, boiled lobster, and lobster in a rich sauce. The lobster's sweet and delicate flesh is a real delicacy that emphasizes the island's best seafood products.

Milos Island has a diversified eating scene where you may enjoy traditional Greek meals and the finest fish. The island's food will satisfy your taste buds and deliver a wonderful culinary experience, with dishes ranging from comfortable moussaka to juicy grilled fish and tasty octopus.

Popular Restaurants and Tavernas
O! Hamos Taverna (Adamas)
- Location: Adamas, close to the harbor

- Unique Selling Point: This taverna has a wonderful outside dining area where you may enjoy your meal. The ambience is warm and inviting, ideal for a casual eating experience.

- Food: O! Hamos Taverna serves traditional Greek cuisine, with a focus on fish and meat dishes. Their signature dishes include expertly grilled octopus, delicious moussaka, and succulent lamb chops.

- Approximate Cost: A dinner at O! Hamos Taverna normally charges between €20 and €30 per person.

Medousa Restaurant (Pollonia)

- Location: Located in the picturesque town of Pollonia, with amazing sea views.

- Special Features: With its scenic site facing the sea, Medousa Restaurant provides a romantic environment. The relaxing atmosphere enhances the whole eating experience.

- Cuisine: The restaurant specializes on fresh seafood and Mediterranean cuisine. You can have wonderful grilled fish, delectable lobster spaghetti, and savory seafood risotto.

- Estimated Cost: A lunch at Medousa Restaurant should cost between €30 and €40 per person.

Avli Restaurant (Plaka)

- Location: Located in Plaka, Milos' lovely and ancient capital.

- Unique Features: Avli Restaurant has a lovely courtyard setting that creates a typical Greek atmosphere. Diners will enjoy the pleasant environment provided by the outside sitting area.

- Food: Avli Restaurant delivers traditional Greek meals with a contemporary touch. Their menu includes items like as stuffed squid, savory spanakopita (spinach pie), and delicate lamb with yogurt sauce.

- Estimated Price: A dinner at Avli Restaurant typically ranges between €25 and €35 per person.

Archontoula Restaurant (Provatas)

- Location: Provatas Beach is nearby, providing a tranquil and peaceful setting.

Archontoula Restaurant is a family-run taverna recognized for its pleasant and inviting ambiance. It's a great place to relax and have a leisurely supper.

- Cuisine: The restaurant serves traditional Greek and Milos cuisine. Dishes such as freshly grilled fish, classic Milos cheese pie, and substantial rabbit stew are available.

- Estimated Cost: A lunch at Archontoula Restaurant should cost between €20 and €30 per person.

Ergina Restaurant (Plaka)

- Location: Located in Plaka's town square, this restaurant provides a convenient and central eating alternative.

- Unique Features: Ergina Restaurant has a beautiful and romantic atmosphere, particularly on its rooftop patio. You may enjoy panoramic views of the surrounding region from there.

- Food: The restaurant serves a varied menu of Mediterranean and Greek meals with unique twists. There are a variety of alternatives available, including seafood, pasta, and vegetarian cuisine.

- Price Range: A dinner at Ergina Restaurant normally costs between €30 and €40 per person.

These famous restaurants and tavernas on Milos Island provide exceptional dining experiences by combining excellent food, lovely surroundings, and kind hospitality.

Milos Wines and Vineyards

Milos Island is well-known for its long winemaking heritage and distinctive vines producing high-quality wines. Milos wines have particular tastes and qualities due to the volcanic soil and Mediterranean environment of the island. Wine connoisseurs will enjoy exploring the local vineyards and sampling the island's wines.

Here are some key details about Milos wines and vineyards

1. Tours of Wineries
- Several wineries on the island provide guided tours of their vineyards, production facilities, and cellars. These trips include information about the winemaking process, local grape varietals, and the island's winemaking heritage.

- Knowledgeable guides share their winemaking experience and enthusiasm, providing a full insight of the Milos wine business. You may learn about the innovative procedures and strategies used by winemakers to create great wines.

Local Grape Varieties
- The white grape type known as "Assyrtiko" is the most popular indigenous grape variety on Milos Island, and it is highly appreciated for its acidity, minerality, and zesty notes. Milos Assyrtiko wines are noted for their freshness and richness, and they represent the island's terroir.

- Other grape types grown on the island include "Athiri" and "Monemvasia" for white wines, as well as "Mandilaria" and "Voudomato" for red wines. Each grape type adds distinct qualities to the wines, demonstrating the diversity of Milos' viticulture.

Wine Tasting
- Wine tastings at nearby vineyards enable you to experience a wide range of Milos wines and identify your particular favorites. You may enjoy various wines' tastes, smells, and textures while learning about their production and aging procedures.

- Milos wines are distinguished by their bright acidity, lively fruit flavors, and traces of volcanic minerals. Citrus, tropical fruits, white flowers, and herbal overtones may be present in the flavor profile. Some vineyards also make sweet wines and dessert wines, providing a variety of alternatives to satisfy a variety of palates.

Vineyards & Wineries

- A visit to the vineyards and wineries is an opportunity to explore the stunning landscapes where the grapes are grown. Notable vineyards on Milos include Triades, Astarti, and Votsalaki. These vineyards are strategically located in different parts of the island, taking advantage of microclimates and unique terroirs.

- **Triades Winery**, in Plaka, is one of the island's oldest wineries. It is a beautiful location with vineyards surrounded by volcanic cliffs and stunning views of the Aegean Sea. The winery produces a variety of wines such as Assyrtiko, Mandilaria, and dessert wines.

- **Astarti Winery**, located near Pollonia, mixes contemporary winemaking processes with ancient customs. The winery is well-known for its organic vineyards and environmentally friendly winemaking methods. Visitors may sample their wines while taking in magnificent views of the sea.

- **Votsalaki Winery,** situated in Milos' southwest corner, specializes in small-batch wines that represent the island's terroir. The vineyards are farmed organically and biodynamically, producing wines with particular character and purity.

Buying Milos Wines

- Many wineries have on-site shops where you can purchase the wines you've tasted and enjoyed. This allows you to bring home a piece of Milos' winemaking heritage and share it with friends and family.

- Additionally, local wine shops

and markets on the island offer a wide selection of Milos wines. The knowledgeable staff can provide recommendations based on your preferences, ensuring you find the perfect bottles to take home.

Wine Events and Festivals

- Throughout the year, Milos holds a variety of wine festivals and events to celebrate the island's winemaking history. These festivities provide the opportunity to sample a wide variety of Milos wines, complemented by local foods and live music.

- The events highlight the island's strong wine culture and provide opportunities to meet with producers, sommeliers, and other wine aficionados. Participating in these events helps you to broaden your knowledge and enjoyment of Milos wines.

Exploring Milos Island's vineyards and delighting in the distinct tastes of its wines is a must for every wine enthusiast. The mix of volcanic soil, unique grape varietals, and devoted winemakers produces wines that capture the essence of the island's terroir and provide an unforgettable sensory experience.

Shopping and Souvenirs

Milos Island provides a great shopping experience, with a variety of local handicrafts, art, and one-of-a-kind souvenirs allowing you to take a bit of the island's beauty and culture home with you. Here's all you need to know about Milos shopping and souvenirs:

Local Handicrafts and Art

Milos is well-known for its skilled craftsmen who produce magnificent handicrafts and artworks inspired by the island's rich cultural past. Here are some examples of local handicrafts and art:

- Ceramic Art: Milos has a long history of producing ceramic art. You'll discover magnificent ceramic pieces with classic patterns and themes, such as vases, plates, and decorative items. Some stores even provide workshops where you may try your hand at making your own ceramic masterpiece.

- **Handwoven Textiles**: On Milos, traditional handwoven textiles like carpets, tablecloths, and scarves are popular souvenirs. These fabrics have elaborate designs and brilliant colors that represent the creative heritage of the island. Look for establishments that specialize in weaving and encourage local craftsmen to sell their wares.

- **Jewelry:** Milos is well-known for its one-of-a-kind jewelry crafted from volcanic stones, pearls, and sea glass. The patterns are often inspired by the island's natural beauty, combining features like as shells and sea forms. There are both modern and traditional jewelry items available that make for beautiful souvenirs.

- **Paintings & Artwork:** Throughout history, Milos Island has been a sanctuary for artists, drawing painters, sculptors, and other creative persons. Paintings representing the island's landscapes, seascapes, and cultural aspects are on show at art galleries and studios. Exploring these galleries enables you to explore the island's creative skills.

Interesting Souvenirs to Bring Home

When it comes to souvenirs, Milos has a vast selection of one-of-a-kind things that embody the character of the island. Here are some noteworthy alternatives:

- **Sea Sponges:** Milos is well-known for its natural sea sponges, which make wonderful one-of-a-kind and environmentally responsible souvenirs. These sponges are obtained in an environmentally friendly manner and may be used for bathing, cleaning, or as decorative items.

- **Local Food products:** Milos makes a variety of local food items that make great presents. Look for olive oil, honey, fragrant herbs, and locally manufactured cheeses like as the famed "xynotyro" and "mizithra." These delectable goods will help you to remember Milos' flavors long after your stay.

- **Volcanic Rock crafts**: Milos' volcanic setting inspires a variety of volcanic rock crafts. Decorative goods, sculptures, and jewelry made from lava stones or pumice serve as one-of-a-kind memories of the island's natural grandeur.

- **Traditional products:** Look for traditional goods that represent the cultural legacy of the island. These may include hand-painted symbols, embroidered goods, handcrafted soaps, and local beverages such as the traditional liqueur "rakomelo."

Consider visiting local markets, boutique stores, and artisan workshops while looking for souvenirs on Milos. Interact with the merchants and craftspeople, who may give information about the items and their cultural value. Remember to support local companies and choose sustainable and genuine souvenirs that reflect your tastes and beliefs.

Bringing home, a piece of Milos via its handicrafts, art, and one-of-a-kind souvenirs enables you to retain your visit's memories while also sharing the island's beauty and workmanship with others.

Entertainment and Nightlife

Milos Island has a dynamic nightlife scene where you may relax, interact, and immerse yourself in the colorful environment of the island. There are several places to spend the nights on Milos, ranging from pubs and beach clubs to traditional music and dance. Here's all you need to know about the island's nightlife and entertainment.

Beach Clubs and Bars

Milos has a wide range of pubs and beach clubs to suit all tastes and inclinations. You'll find alternatives to fit your mood, whether you're seeking for a calm coastal place or a vibrant venue to dance the night away. Here are some of Milos' most popular pubs and beach clubs:

Salt: Salt is a fashionable beach bar in Pollonia noted for its laid-back vibe and magnificent views. Relax on sunbeds while sipping delicious beverages and listening to relaxing music.

Akri: Akri is a famous pub in Adamas with a large outside patio with panoramic views of the port. This sophisticated establishment provides a broad range of beverages, including cocktails, wines, and local spirits, making it an ideal location for mingling and taking in the evening scene.

Aloha: Aloha is a beach club in the center of Adamas that blends a vibrant atmosphere with gorgeous surroundings. Dance to DJ sets, drink on inventive cocktails, and enjoy the seaside location while socializing and dancing the night away.

Utopia Cafe Bar: Utopia is a wonderful cafe bar with a pleasant ambiance located in Plaka. This establishment is well-known for its unique drinks, friendly service, and sometimes live music events. It's a terrific location to unwind and enjoy the evening in Plaka's gorgeous surroundings.

Enigma: Enigma, located in Pollonia, is a popular venue for live music and entertainment. This tavern organizes Greek music evenings on a regular basis, with local artists singing traditional songs. Immerse yourself in the vibrant environment, dance to Greek rhythms, and have a genuine cultural experience.

Traditional Music and Dancing

Milos Island has a wide variety of nightlife and entertainment alternatives to suit a wide range of tastes and interests. The island provides something for everyone, whether you're seeking for lively beach bars, traditional music, and dance, or cultural events. Here's a full look into Milos' nightlife and entertainment:

Traditional Music and Dance

- **Taverna nights**: Throughout the island, several traditional tavernas offer special nights where you can enjoy live Greek music and traditional dance. These events provide a one-of-a-kind chance to experience Greek culture and hospitality while dining on delectable Greek food. Local musicians and dancers perform traditional Greek dances, resulting in a vibrant and joyful scene.

- **Festivals & Events:** Throughout the year, Milos holds a variety of cultural festivals and events that provide opportunity to see traditional music and dance. These events highlight the island's cultural history and often include performances by local artists. Traditional music, dance, and cultural displays may be found in festivals such as the Milos Mining Museum Festival and the Festival of Agia Marina.

- **Milos Folklore Museum:** The Milos Folklore Museum, situated in the hamlet of Plaka, is an excellent venue to learn about the island's cultural heritage, including music and dance. The museum has a collection of folklore and local tradition-related musical instruments, costumes, and artifacts. You may also view videos of traditional dances and learn about their importance in Milos' culture.

On Milos Island, you may enjoy a varied and diverse nightlife experience by exploring the pubs, beach clubs, traditional tavernas, and cultural events. Immerse yourself in the bright music, dance to traditional rhythms, and enjoy the lively environment of the island as you make wonderful memories of your stay on Milos.

Cultural and Historical Experiences

Milos Island provides a variety of cultural and historical activities that enable tourists to immerse themselves in its rich past and traditional festivals and events. Here are some of the noteworthy experiences available on the island

Traditional Festivals and Events

- Festival of Agia Marina: Held on July 17th in Klima, the Festival of Agia Marina is a prominent religious feast. Religious processions, rites, and feasts are held in honor of Agia Marina, the village's patron saint. Locals and tourists alike gather to venerate the saint, perform traditional dances and music, and eat excellent local food. It's a bustling festival that highlights the island's religious traditions and cultural history.

- **Milos Mining Museum Festival:** The Milos Mining Museum Festival is held each year in mid-August at Adamas' Mining Museum. This cultural event honors the island's mining heritage and provides visitors with the opportunity to learn about mining processes and the importance of mining in the local economy. The event includes mining-related displays, talks, and demonstrations, as well as traditional music performances and local food booths. It's a chance to learn about Milos' industrial history and enjoy the island's rich mining heritage.

- **Cultural exhibits:** Milos hosts a number of cultural exhibits that highlight the island's archaeological riches and historical items. The Adamas Archaeological Museum includes an incredible collection of ancient antiquities, including ceramics, sculptures, and the famed Venus de Milo statue. The museum offers an enlightening look into the island's past cultures and creative accomplishments. Furthermore, the Plaka Ecclesiastical Museum exhibits holy icons, vestments, and artifacts, showcasing the island's religious art and tradition.

Participating in cultural activities and attending traditional festivals enables you to observe the island's customs, traditions, and creative manifestations. These encounters deepen one's awareness of Milos' cultural and historical importance, providing a window into the island's history and present. Immerse yourself in the lively celebrations, marvel at the interesting displays, and appreciate Milos' rich cultural tapestry.

Etiquette and Local Customs

When visiting Milos Island, it is necessary to get acquainted with the local traditions and etiquette in order to have a polite and pleasurable experience. Here are some of Milos' most important traditions and etiquette:

- Greetings: The people of Milos are kind and inviting. When entering businesses, restaurants, or meeting people, it is usual to greet them with a cheerful "Yasou" (hello) or "Kalimera" (good morning). Handshakes are the most usual type of greeting, however, close friends and relatives may share cheek kisses.

- **Respect for Churches**: Milos is home to a number of churches and monasteries that are both religious and culturally significant. It is usual to dress modestly and abstain from loud talks or bad conduct while approaching these hallowed areas. It is also courteous to remove caps and sunglasses and to take photos without upsetting worshipers.

- **Hospitality:** On the island, hospitality is strongly prized, and inhabitants take delight in welcoming guests. It is usual to offer a little gift, such as a bottle of local wine or a box of chocolates when welcomed to someone's house. Accepting the given beverages and conversing demonstrates gratitude for their hospitality.

- **Dining Etiquette**: It is traditional to wait for the host to ask you to sit down and begin the meal while eating at a restaurant or in someone's home. It is customary to sample a little bit of everything given and to complement the host's food. Tipping is popular in Milos, and a 10-15% tip is appreciated for excellent service.

Milos Folklore

Milos Island has a rich folklore and customs that the local population still celebrates and cherishes. These traditional rituals provide a rare glimpse into the island's history and customs. Here are some prominent Milian folklore and traditions:

- **Traditional Dances:** Milos has a thriving folk dance tradition called as "balos" or "kantades," which include rhythmic movements and expressive gestures accompanied by traditional music. You may be able to observe and perhaps participate in these exciting dance performances during festivals and special events.

- **Costumes & Festive Attire:** Milos' folklore and cultural festivals are heavily reliant on traditional costumes. Colorful costumes embellished with elaborate embroidery and lace are often worn by ladies, while traditional vests and pants are worn by males. These costumes offer a sense of elegance and ethnic pride to festivals, weddings, and other traditional celebrations.

- **Religious Festivals**: Religious festivals are important in Milos' customs. Through processions, rituals, and feasts, these activities bring communities together to celebrate saints and religious luminaries. The celebrations are distinguished by colorful décor, music, traditional dances, and regional specialties. Participating in these ceremonies enables you to see the island's religious dedication and feeling of community.

You may develop a greater appreciation for the island's cultural history and connect with its hospitable people by observing local customs and etiquette and immersing yourself in Milos' folklore and traditions. Accept the conventions, interact with the people, and enjoy the rich tapestry of Milos' customs and traditions.

Outdoor Activities and Sports
Hiking and Nature Trails

Milos Island has a beautiful scenery and a diversified natural beauties, making it a perfect destination for hikers and nature lovers. Hiking the island's paths enables you to immerse yourself in the breathtaking scenery, uncover hidden jewels, and enjoy the untamed environment. What you should know about hiking and nature paths in Milos:

- **Guided Tours:** While many hiking routes may be explored on your own, attending a guided tour might improve your experience. Knowledgeable guides may give significant insights into the island's flora, wildlife, and geological aspects while also ensuring your safety and assisting you in navigating the paths. Guided excursions are especially advised for difficult or distant routes where local knowledge is useful.

- **Price:** The price of guided hiking trips in Milos varies according to length, difficulty level, and inclusions. A half-day excursion normally costs between €30 and €60 per person. Full-day trips and specialty hiking experiences may be more expensive. For the most accurate and up-to-date prices, check with local tour operators or agencies.

- **Packing Essentials:** When going on a hiking or nature path experience in Milos, make sure to include the following items:

- Sturdy and comfortable hiking boots or shoes for traversing difficult terrain.

- Weather-appropriate apparel that is lightweight and breathable.

- Sun protection, such as a hat, sunscreen, and sunglasses, since the paths may provide little shade.

- Plenty of water to remain hydrated during the trek.

- Snacks or a packed lunch, since food choices may be limited along the routes.

- A compact backpack for basics such as a map, camera, and personal stuff.

- Best Time of Day: Hiking or nature trails in Milos are best experienced in the early morning or late afternoon. The temperatures are gentler at these periods, and the lighting is typically ideal for capturing the magnificence of the countryside. Hiking should be avoided during the warmest hours of the day to avoid heat fatigue and to have a more pleasurable experience.

Popular Hiking paths

Milos has a range of hiking paths to suit all ability levels and interests. Among the most popular trails are:

- **Milos Catacombs walk:** This walk leads through gorgeous scenery to the ancient catacombs, providing insight into Milos' rich past.

- **Kleftiko walk**: Beginning in Agios Ioannis, this walk leads to the enthralling sea caves and rock formations of Kleftiko.

- **Profitis Ilias Trail:** Climb to Milos' highest mountain for panoramic views of the island and the Aegean Sea.

- **Papafragas Trail:** Explore the stunning coastal cliffs as well as the hidden jewel of Papafragas Beach, which is noted for its turquoise seas.

Hiking or nature path adventures in Milos allow you to completely experience the island's natural marvels, breathe in the fresh air, and find hidden treasures. Be prepared, respect the environment, and experience the beauty that reveals with each step whether you walk alone or join a guided trip.

Snorkeling and Scuba Diving

Milos Island has a rich underwater environment and crystal-clear seas, making it an ideal location for scuba divers and snorkelers. Exploring the underwater environment of Milos is an amazing experience, whether you're a seasoned diver or a beginning snorkeler. Here's what you should know:

- Scuba Diver

- Guided Tours: Joining a guided tour is advised if you are new to scuba diving or wish to visit the greatest diving areas. Dive instructors are trained to take you through underwater landscapes, guarantee your safety, and give information on marine life and geological structures.

- Price: The cost of scuba diving in Milos varies based on criteria like as length, number of dives, equipment rental, and whether or not a guide is included. Prices normally vary between €50 and €100 per dive. Diving packages or courses may provide discounts. It's best to check with local diving shops for particular price information.

- Equipment: Most dive shops in Milos supply scuba diving equipment such as wetsuits, masks, fins, regulators, and tanks. If you have your own diving equipment, you may bring it with you for a more comfortable and familiar diving experience.

- Certification: If you aren't already a qualified diver, Milos provides options to become one via numerous dive facilities and organizations. Completing a certification course will enable you to delve deeper and independently in the future.

Snorkeling

- Accessibility: Snorkeling is a popular and accessible hobby that people of all ages and ability levels may enjoy. Milos' coastline is dotted with snorkeling opportunities, ranging from widely accessible beaches to secluded coves.

- **Snorkeling equipment** is basic, consisting of a snorkel, mask, and fins. If you don't have your own equipment, you may rent it from seaside stores or water sports facilities.

- Snorkeling Locations

- **Sarakiniko Beach:** Explore the moon-like landscape's underwater rock formations and swim amid schools of colorful fish.

- Kleftiko: Snorkel in Kleftiko's beautiful waters to find secret sea caves and fascinating marine life.

- **Gerakas**: With its quiet and translucent waters, this isolated beach provides great snorkeling chances, enabling you to witness a variety of marine animals.

- **Safety:** When snorkeling, always put your safety first. Select snorkeling locations that are acceptable for your ability level, swim within your boundaries, and be mindful of any currents or underwater dangers. It's also a good idea to snorkel with a companion and adhere to basic snorkeling safety precautions.

- **greatest Time of Day:** The greatest time for scuba diving and snorkeling in Milos is usually in the morning or early afternoon when the seas are calmest and visibility is optimum. However, since conditions may change based on weather and tide patterns, it's best to check with local diving facilities or snorkeling operators for the best periods.

You will get the chance to experience the colorful marine life, explore underwater caverns, and view the beauty of Milos from a fresh perspective by diving under the surface of the sea. Milos provides a plethora of underwater adventures for all water lovers, whether you prefer scuba diving to explore deeper depths or snorkeling to enjoy the shallow coastal regions.

Windsurfing and kitesurfing

Milos Island is a windsurfing and kitesurfing paradise due to its ideal wind conditions, gorgeous beaches, and expansive coastlines. Whether you're a seasoned rider or a novice seeking to experience these adrenaline-water sports, Milos has plenty of options. Here's what you should know:

- **Accessibility:** Windsurfing and kitesurfing are popular sports on Milos' beaches, with Adamas, Paleochori, and Achivadolimni being popular destinations. These beaches provide plenty of space, good wind directions, and appropriate water conditions for windsurfers and kitesurfers of all ability levels.

- **Equipment Rental:** If you don't possess windsurfing or kitesurfing equipment, you may rent it at water sports establishments near the beaches. They sell a wide range of equipment, such as windsurfing boards, sails, kites, harnesses, and safety equipment. Rental rates might range from €20 to €50 per hour based on the length and kind of equipment.

- **Lessons and Guided Tours:** If you're new to windsurfing or kitesurfing, taking lessons from licensed instructors is strongly advised. These classes will teach you the skills, tactics, and safety information you need to enjoy sports safely. For novices and those wishing to enhance their abilities, many water sports facilities provide classes and guided trips. Lessons may cost between €50 and €100 for each session, depending on length and group number.

- **Wind Conditions:** Milos is well-known for its good wind conditions, especially in the summer. The Meltemi wind, a constant northern wind, produces great conditions for windsurfing and kitesurfing. Wind speeds often vary from 15 to 30 knots, making for exhilarating rides and the ability to do leaps, stunts, and maneuvers.

- Safety Considerations: Windsurfing and kitesurfing are physically demanding sports that need certain skills and safety procedures. It is critical to analyze your talents and choose appropriate locations and equipment for your ability level. Wearing a life jacket or harness, utilizing suitable safety leashes, and being mindful of other water users are all important safety precautions. Be aware of the wind direction, tides, and any possible risks in the water.

- Best Time of Day: The best time of day for windsurfing and kitesurfing in Milos is often mid-morning to early afternoon. The wind is usually at its greatest during this time of year, making these water activities excellent. Wind patterns might change, so check the local weather forecast and get guidance from experienced riders or water sports establishments to identify the optimum time to hit the water.

- Packing Essentials: When planning a windsurfing or kitesurfing trip, keep the following items in mind:

- Sun protection swimwear and rash guards

- Water shoes or booties to keep your feet safe.

- Sunscreen and a hat for protection from the sun

- A towel and clothing to change into after the session

- Snacks and water for hydration

You may enjoy the excitement of windsurfing or kitesurfing while admiring the natural beauty of Milos by taking advantage of the island's outstanding wind conditions. Milos is a great location for windsurfing and kitesurfing aficionados, whether you're a seasoned rider or a novice, thanks to its magnificent beaches, consistent winds, and competent training.

Yoga and Wellness Retreats

Milos Island offers a tranquil and beautiful location for yoga and health retreats, enabling participants to reconnect with themselves, achieve inner peace, and refresh their minds, body, and soul. Here's all you need to know about Milos yoga and health retreats:

- **Retreat establishments:** Several retreat establishments on the island provide specialized yoga and health rooms and programs. These facilities are often located in serene settings, offering a calm environment for relaxation and self-reflection. They often include large yoga studios, meditation rooms, outside gardens, and nice lodging alternatives.

- **Yoga Styles and Courses:** Retreat facilities on Milos provide a wide range of yoga styles and courses for practitioners of all levels. Whether you're a novice or an experienced yogi, you can discover Hatha, Vinyasa, Yin, Ashtanga, and more courses. Experienced teachers often lead the programs, guiding participants through a variety of yoga postures, breathing exercises, and meditation activities.

- **wellbeing Activities:** In addition to yoga, many retreats include a comprehensive approach to well-being, including meditation, sound therapy, mindfulness workshops, and nature walks. These exercises are designed to enhance relaxation, self-awareness, and general health and well-being. Additional wellness activities such as spa treatments, massages, and nutritional courses may be available at certain retreats.

- **Retreat Packages:** Retreat packages may last anywhere from a few days to many weeks. They often include lodging, yoga and health sessions, meals, and, on occasion, transportation or airport transfers. Retreat package prices might vary based on the length, style of lodging, and a number of inclusions. It is best to contact the retreat facilities directly for precise information and prices.

- Appropriate for All Levels: Yoga and wellness vacations on Milos are appropriate for practitioners of all levels, including novices. Whether you're new to yoga or have a long-standing practice, the teachers at the retreat facilities are competent in tailoring lessons to individual requirements and making changes as needed. This fosters a positive and welcoming atmosphere for all participants.

- Best Time to Visit: Milos is famed for its warm temperature, which makes it ideal for yoga and health retreats all year. However, the summer months of May to September are especially popular due to the warm and sunny weather. Spring and fall shoulder seasons may also be excellent times to visit, with moderate weather and fewer people.

- Personal Needs: When preparing for a yoga and health retreat, keep the following items in mind:

- Yoga gear that is comfortable and a yoga mat (although some retreat locations may offer mats).

- A hat and sunscreen for outdoor activities

- Clothing that is lightweight and breathable during hot weather

- A reusable water bottle to keep yourself hydrated

- Personal toiletries and any drugs necessary

Milos yoga and wellness retreats provide a tranquil respite from the demands of daily life, enabling you to concentrate on self-care, self-discovery, and personal development. Milos offers a great background for feeding your body, mind, and soul via yoga, meditation, and holistic wellness practices, with its gorgeous scenery, quiet environment, and specialized retreat facilities.

Day Trips and Surrounding Islands
Kimolos Island Excursions

Kimolos Island, only a short distance from Milos, is a wonderful day trip or excursion location. Kimolos, known for its natural beauty and serene ambiance, provides a pleasant respite from the larger tourist sites. Here's everything you need to know about Kimolos excursions:

- Getting There: From Milos, you may take a ferry or a boat trip to Kimolos. Ferries run frequently between the two islands, with a 30-minute passage time. You may also take a guided boat tour that includes visits to both Milos and Kimolos.

- **Chorio, the Capital:** Chorio, the major town of Kimolos, is a lovely village with typical Cycladic architecture. The village has small cobblestone alleys, whitewashed cottages with colorful doors and windows, and attractive squares where you may rest and take in the tranquil atmosphere.

- **immaculate Beaches:** Kimolos is known for its immaculate beaches and blue seas. Aliki, Psathi, and Bonatsa are some of the most popular beaches. These beaches provide a tranquil setting for sunbathing, swimming, and snorkeling. The beaches' uncrowded character adds to its allure, enabling you to relax and appreciate the natural beauty without disturbances.

- **Geological Phenomena:** Kimolos, like its neighboring island Milos, has a rich geological history and intriguing rock formations. The island is famous for its distinctive volcanic terrain, which has colorful cliffs, caverns, and rock formations. Exploring these geological formations adds an element of adventure to your day trip, with hiking and photographic possibilities.

- **Local food**: While visiting Kimolos, be sure to enjoy the island's delectable food. Traditional Greek cuisine created with fresh, local ingredients are available at the local tavernas and eateries. To try,

try "louza" (cured pig), "manoura" cheese, and "pitarakia" (local cheese pies). Don't miss out on the island's famed "amygdalota" almond desserts.

- Kimolos is well-known for its local handicrafts and artisanal items. Shops providing traditional pottery, handcrafted jewelry, textiles, and woven baskets may be found on Chorio's tiny lanes. These one-of-a-kind mementos are excellent memories or presents for loved ones back home.

Visit to Polyaigos Island

Polyaigos, also known as Polyaegos, is a tiny deserted island off Milos' northeast shore. Polyaigos provides a totally unique and private experience, with its beautiful beaches, crystal-clear seas, and undisturbed natural beauty. Here's what you should know:

- **Boat Excursions:** The most common way to see Polyaigos is to join a boat trip or hire a private boat. Several travel providers on Milos provide day excursions to Polyaigos, including transportation and supervision. The boat excursion usually includes stops at several beaches and coves throughout the island, enabling you to see the island's natural treasures.

- **Pristine Beaches & Bays:** Polyaigos is famous for its beautiful beaches and quiet bays. Sarakiniko, Ammoudaraki, and Fykiada are just a few of the island's unspoilt sandy beaches. These beaches provide a calm and relaxing ambiance, with brilliant blue seas ideal for swimming and snorkeling. Some beaches may have limited amenities, so pack food, drink, and any other supplies you may need.

- **Natural Beauty:** Polyaigos is a naturally protected species.

One of the reserve's greatest draws is its pristine beauty. The island is known for its craggy cliffs, stunning rock formations, and rich flora and wildlife. Explore the island's hiking paths and marvel at the gorgeous scenery, including spectacular vistas across the Aegean Sea.

- **Wildlife and Birdwatching**: Polyaigos has a diverse marine ecology as well as a number of bird species. Several seabirds, including the uncommon Eleonora's falcon, nest on the island. Nature lovers and birdwatchers will enjoy seeing the island's fauna and birds in their natural environment.

Serifos and Sifnos Boat Trips

Serifos and Sifnos are two nearby islands that may be visited by boat from Milos. Both islands have their own distinct personality, historical landmarks, attractive towns, and beautiful beaches. What you should know about boat journeys to Serifos and Sifnos:

- **Getting There:** Regular ferry services link Milos with Serifos and Sifnos, making day trips to these islands possible. The length of the boat ride will vary based on the route and sailing timetables. It is best to verify boat schedules ahead of time and prepare appropriately.

- **Serifos:** Known for its classic Cycladic buildings and stunning beaches, Serifos provides a relaxed environment and a taste of true island life. Discover Chora, the principal town, with its small alleys, whitewashed buildings, and attractive squares. Visit the historic Serifos Castle on the island's highest point for panoramic views. Enjoy the island's beaches, which are recognized for their crystal-clear seas and tranquil atmosphere, such as Livadi, Livadakia, and Psili Ammos.

- **Sifnos:** The Greek Island of Sifnos is famous for its rich history, cultural legacy, and gastronomic pleasures. Discover the lovely settlements of the island, like as Apollonia, Kastro, and Artemonas, with their traditional architecture and pleasant ambiance. Visit the historic Monastery of Panagia Chrissopigi, the island's icon. Don't miss out on sampling Sifnos' traditional food, which is noted for its delectable local specialties like as chickpea soup, mastello cheese, and honey-drenched almond desserts.

- Activities and Sightseeing: Aside from touring the towns and beaches, both Serifos and Sifnos offer outdoor activities and sightseeing. Hike picturesque paths, see historic ruins and archaeological sites, and participate in water sports and beach activities. Each island has its own distinct set of sights and sites that highlight its cultural and historical importance.

- Guided Tours: While exploring Serifos and Sifnos on your own is doable, taking a guided tour or hiring a local guide may improve your experience. Guided tours give informative commentary, guarantee you see the attractions of each island, and provide transportation and logistics.

- ideal Time to Visit: From May through September, the ideal time to visit Serifos, Sifnos, and other adjacent islands is during the summer months, when the weather is nice and the tourist facilities are fully operating. Visiting during the shoulder seasons of spring and fall, on the other hand, may provide great weather and less tourists.

- Price and Duration: The price of a boat voyage to Serifos and Sifnos varies based on the ferry company, route, and ticket type. It's a good idea to double-check the costs and timetables ahead of time. The length of the day excursion will be determined by the amount of time allotted for exploring each island as well as the boat timetables.

CHAPTER FIVE
Itinerary Suggestions
7 days itinerary for first-timers
Day 1
- Arrival in Milos: Accommodation costs vary depending on your preferences and budget. Budget accommodations start at around $50 per night, while mid-range options range from $80 to $150 per night. Luxury accommodations can go up to $300 or more per night.

Day 2
- Boat Trip to Kleftiko: Joining a boat tour to Kleftiko costs around $40 to $60 per person, depending on the duration and inclusions. Some tours provide lunch or snacks on board. Don't forget to bring some cash for additional expenses such as drinks or equipment rentals.

Day 3
- South Coast Beaches: There are no entrance fees for the beaches, but renting sunbeds and umbrellas may cost around $10 to $15 per set. Enjoying a meal at a beachfront taverna can cost between $15 to $30 per person, depending on your choice of dishes.

Day 4
- Discovering Milos' History: Entrance to the ancient theater of Milos and the Catacombs of Milos costs around $4 to $6 per person. The admission fee for the Mining Museum is approximately $5 per person.

Day 5
- Day Trip to Kimolos: Ferry tickets from Milos to Kimolos cost around $15 to $20 round trip. Exploring the island of Kimolos is

free, but you may need to budget for meals and drinks at local restaurants, which range from $15 to $30 per person.

Day 6

- Outdoor Adventure: Hiking trails in Milos are free of charge. If you plan to rent scuba diving or snorkeling equipment, it can cost approximately $30 to $50 per person for a half-day rental. Guided scuba diving tours start at around $70 per person.

Day 7

- Polyaigos and Serifos: Boat trips to Polyaigos and Serifos can range from $50 to $80 per person, depending on the duration and inclusions. Lunch or snacks may be provided on board. Expenses on Serifos, such as meals and drinks, are similar to those in Milos.

This itinerary provides a general idea of the estimated costs involved. Adjustments can be made based on your preferences, budget, and the duration of your stay in Milos.

3-day itinerary for first-time visitors to Milos

Day 1:

- Morning: Arrive in Milos and check into your accommodation. Spend the morning exploring the charming town of Plaka, known for its narrow streets, traditional Cycladic architecture, and stunning views. Visit the Archaeological Museum of Milos to learn about the island's history and ancient artifacts.

- Afternoon: Head to Sarakiniko Beach, a unique moon-like landscape with white volcanic rock formations. Enjoy the surreal surroundings, take memorable photos, and swim in the turquoise waters. Relax on the beach and soak up the sun.

- Evening: Dine at a local taverna in Plaka or nearby Adamas, where you can savor traditional Greek dishes such as moussaka, souvlaki, or fresh seafood. Sample local wines and indulge in a delicious meal.

Day 2:

- Morning: Take a boat trip to Kleftiko, a stunning sea cave complex on the southwest coast of Milos. Explore the caves, swim in the crystal-clear waters, and marvel at the majestic rock formations. Enjoy snorkeling or diving in this breathtaking underwater world.

- Afternoon: Visit the picturesque fishing village of Klima, known for its colorful boathouses called "Syrmata." Take a leisurely stroll along the waterfront, admire the unique architecture, and learn about the island's maritime heritage.

- Evening: Enjoy a romantic sunset at Plathiena Beach. Relax on the golden sand, dip your toes in the crystal-clear waters, and witness the sky turning shades of orange and pink as the sun sets. Consider having a picnic dinner on the beach or dine at a nearby taverna.

Day 3:

- Morning: Embark on a hiking adventure to the highest point on Milos, Profitis Ilias Mountain. Enjoy panoramic views of the island, its coastline, and the surrounding Aegean Sea. Pack water, snacks, and sun protection for the hike.

- Afternoon: Visit the charming village of Pollonia, a tranquil fishing village known for its relaxed atmosphere and beautiful beach. Spend some time exploring the village, lounging on the beach, or indulging in water sports such as paddleboarding or kayaking.

- Evening: Experience traditional Greek music and dancing at a local taverna in Pollonia or Adamas. Immerse yourself in the lively atmosphere, learn some traditional dance moves, and enjoy the local music performances.

Note: This itinerary provides a general overview of the activities and attractions you can explore during a three-day visit to Milos. You can adjust the itinerary based on your preferences and interests. It's recommended to check the opening hours and availability of boat tours, hikes, and cultural events ahead of time.

A family-friendly five-day itinerary for your trip to Milos

Day 1:
- Morning: Arrive in Milos and settle into your accommodation.

- Afternoon: Head to Papafragas Beach, a hidden gem with crystal-clear waters and a small cove, perfect for families. Spend the afternoon swimming, snorkeling, and building sandcastles. Cost: Free.

- Evening: Dine at a local taverna in Adamas, where you can enjoy a variety of Greek dishes. Estimated cost: €40-€60 for a family of four.

Day 2:
- Morning: Explore the Catacombs of Milos, an ancient underground burial site. Take a guided tour to learn about the history and significance of the catacombs. Estimated cost: €5 per person.

- Afternoon: Visit the Archaeological Museum of Milos in Plaka. Admire the ancient artifacts and learn about the island's rich history. Estimated cost: €3 per person.

- Evening: Enjoy a relaxing dinner at a waterfront restaurant in Pollonia, offering fresh seafood and Greek specialties. Estimated cost: €50-€70 for a family of four.

Day 3:

- Morning: Take a boat tour to Kleftiko, a stunning sea cave complex. Explore the caves, swim in the crystal-clear waters, and enjoy snorkeling. Estimated cost: €50-€70 per person for a guided boat tour.

- Afternoon: Visit the Milos Mining Museum in Adamas to learn about the island's mining heritage. Discover the fascinating world of minerals and mining techniques. Estimated cost: €3 per person.

- Evening: Enjoy a family-friendly dinner at a traditional taverna in Plaka, offering a variety of Greek dishes. Estimated cost: €40-€60 for a family of four.

Day 4:

- Morning: Visit the Ancient Theatre of Milos and admire the historic site. Take in the panoramic views of the surrounding area. Estimated cost: Free.

- Afternoon: Spend the day at Paliochori Beach, known for its thermal springs. Relax on the beach and enjoy the warm waters. Estimated cost: Free.

- Evening: Have a barbecue picnic at Tsigrado Beach. Bring your own food and enjoy a family meal in this secluded and picturesque location. Estimated cost: €20-€30 for food supplies.

Day 5:

- Morning: Join a guided hiking tour to explore Milos' natural beauty. Choose a family-friendly trail that suits your fitness level. Estimated cost: €20-€30 per person for a guided tour.

- Afternoon: Explore the charming village of Pollonia. Visit the Folklore Museum of Milos to learn about local traditions and customs. Estimated cost: €3 per person.

- Evening: Have a farewell dinner at a restaurant in Adamas, trying out local delicacies and enjoying the lively atmosphere. Estimated cost: €50-€70 for a family of four.

Note: The estimated costs are approximate and can vary depending on the specific establishments and services you choose. It's recommended to allocate a budget for meals, activities, and transportation based on your family's preferences and needs.

5 days adrenaline-pumping itinerary for your adventurous trip to Milos.

Day 1:
- Morning: Arrive in Milos and settle into your accommodation.

- Afternoon: Rent ATVs or mountain bikes and explore the rugged landscapes of Milos. Ride through off-road trails and enjoy the adrenaline rush. Estimated cost: €40-€60 per ATV or bike rental.

- Evening: Dine at a local taverna in Adamas, where you can replenish your energy with hearty Greek cuisine. Estimated cost: €40-€60 for a meal for two.

Day 2:
- Morning: Join a guided rock-climbing excursion in the Kleftiko area. Scale the impressive cliffs and experience the thrill of climbing in a stunning natural setting. Estimated cost: €80-€100 per person for a guided rock-climbing tour.

- Afternoon: Take a boat tour to discover the sea caves and snorkel in the crystal-clear waters of Milos. Enjoy the underwater beauty and explore hidden caves. Estimated cost: €50-€70 per person for a guided boat tour.

- Evening: Grab dinner at a beachfront restaurant in Pollonia, where you can unwind and enjoy delicious seafood. Estimated cost: €50-€70 for a meal for two.

Day 3:

- Morning: Embark on a thrilling scuba diving adventure. Discover the vibrant underwater world of Milos, with its diverse marine life and underwater rock formations. Estimated cost: €80-€100 per person for a scuba diving experience.

- Afternoon: Try your hand at windsurfing or kitesurfing in one of the windy spots on the island. Feel the rush as you glide across the water and ride the waves. Estimated cost: €40-€60 per person for windsurfing or kitesurfing rental.

- Evening: Enjoy a relaxing dinner at a traditional taverna in Plaka, where you can savor Greek specialties and unwind after an action-packed day. Estimated cost: €40-€60 for a meal for two.

Day 4:

- Morning: Go on a canyoning adventure in the island's ravines. Descend waterfalls, jump into natural pools, and navigate through the canyons for an adrenaline-filled experience. Estimated cost: €80-€100 per person for a guided canyoning tour.

- Afternoon: Rent a kayak or paddleboard and explore the coastline of Milos at your own pace. Discover hidden coves and caves while enjoying the thrill of paddling on the open water. Estimated cost: €40-€60 per kayak or paddleboard rental.

- Evening: Have a barbecue dinner at a scenic spot overlooking the sea. Bring your own supplies or purchase them from local markets. Estimated cost: €20-€30 for food supplies.

Day 5:

- Morning: Join a guided hiking or trail running tour to explore Milos' diverse landscapes. Traverse scenic trails, conquer challenging terrains, and experience the thrill of outdoor adventure. Estimated cost: €20-€30 per person for a guided hiking or trail running tour.

- Afternoon: Visit Sarakiniko Beach, known for its unique moon-like landscape. Spend the afternoon cliff diving, snorkeling, or simply enjoying the stunning surroundings. Estimated cost: Free.

- Evening: Indulge in a celebratory dinner at a top-rated restaurant in Adamas, treating yourself to gourmet dishes and local delicacies. Estimated cost: €80-€100 for a meal for two.

Practical Information and Tips
General packing essentials
1. Clothing and Accessories:
- Lightweight and breathable clothing for warm weather (shorts, t-shirts, dresses)

- Swimwear and beach cover-ups

- Comfortable walking shoes or sandals

- Hat or cap to protect from the sun

- Sunglasses

- Lightweight jacket or sweater for cooler evenings

- Beach towel

- Undergarments and socks

- Sleepwear

2. Toiletries and Personal Care:
- Sunscreen with a high SPF

- Insect repellent

- Toiletries (toothbrush, toothpaste, shampoo, conditioner, soap)

- Medications and any necessary prescriptions

- First aid kit (band-aids, antiseptic ointment, pain relievers)

- Hand sanitizer

- Travel-sized toiletries for convenience

3. Electronics and Documentation:
- Mobile phone and charger

- Camera or video recorder

- Power adapter (if needed)

- Travel documents (passport, identification, travel insurance, boarding passes)

- Printed copies of important documents (hotel reservations, itinerary, emergency contact numbers)

4. Beach and Outdoor Essentials:
- Beach bag or backpack

- Snorkeling gear (if you have your own)

- Water shoes or sandals for rocky beaches

- Waterproof phone case or pouch

- Beach umbrella or shade tent

- Picnic blanket or beach mat

- Reusable water bottle

5. Miscellaneous:
- Money and/or credit cards

- Travel guidebook or maps

- Portable charger or power bank

- Travel pillow and eye mask for comfort during transportation

- Reusable shopping bag for souvenirs

- Entertainment items (books, magazines, playing cards)

Remember to pack according to the specific season and weather conditions during your visit to Milos. It's always a good idea to check the local forecast before packing to ensure you have the appropriate clothing and essentials for a comfortable trip.

General safety tips
1. Personal Safety:
- Be aware of your surroundings and trust your instincts.

- Avoid walking alone in unfamiliar or poorly lit areas, especially at night.

- Keep your personal belongings secure and be cautious of pickpockets in crowded areas.

- Keep important documents (passport, ID, etc.) and valuables in a safe place (hotel safe, money belt).

- Stay hydrated and protect yourself from the sun by wearing sunscreen and a hat, especially during hot weather.

- Follow local laws and customs to avoid any legal issues or misunderstandings.

2. Transportation Safety:
- Use licensed and reputable transportation services.

- Wear seatbelts in cars and helmets when riding motorcycles or bicycles.

- Follow traffic rules and exercise caution when crossing roads.

- If renting a vehicle, familiarize yourself with local driving regulations and road conditions.

3. Water Safety:
- Observe and follow any posted beach safety signs and warnings.

- Swim in designated areas with lifeguards present.

- Be cautious of strong currents and changing tides.

- If participating in water activities, such as snorkeling or diving, ensure you have the necessary skills and equipment.

4. Health and Medical Safety:

- Carry a basic first aid kit with essential items like band-aids, antiseptic ointment, and any necessary medications.

- Drink bottled water or use a water purification system to avoid drinking contaminated water.

- Follow proper hygiene practices, such as washing hands regularly.

- If you have any pre-existing medical conditions, bring necessary medications and inform your travel companions of any allergies or medical concerns.

5. Emergency Preparedness:
- Save emergency contact numbers for local authorities, your embassy or consulate, and your accommodations.

- Familiarize yourself with the location of the nearest medical facilities and emergency services.

- Share your itinerary with a trusted person and check in with them periodically.

- Keep important documents and copies of them (passport, ID, travel insurance) in a safe place.

Remember that these are general safety tips, and it's always recommended to research specific safety guidelines and considerations for your destination. Adhering to these safety tips can help ensure a smooth and enjoyable trip while minimizing potential risks or emergencies.

20 do's and don'ts based on local customs and etiquette in Milos, Greece

Do's:

1. Greet people with a warm "Kalimera" (Good morning) or "Kalispera" (Good evening) when you meet them.

2. Show respect and courtesy to elders, as age is highly respected in Greek culture.

3. Dress modestly when visiting churches or religious sites, covering shoulders and knees.

4. Say "Efharisto" (Thank you) when receiving hospitality or assistance.

5. Try to learn a few basic Greek phrases and use them when interacting with locals.

6. Embrace the slow-paced lifestyle and enjoy leisurely meals, known as "meze," accompanied by conversation and good company.

7. Take off your shoes when entering someone's home, unless otherwise indicated.

8. Embrace the Greek concept of "philoxenia," which means showing hospitality and generosity to guests.

9. Respect the environment by not littering and disposing of trash properly.

10. Be open to trying traditional Greek cuisine and specialties, such as moussaka, souvlaki, and feta cheese.

Don'ts:

1. Don't interrupt or speak loudly during conversations, as Greeks value good manners and respectful communication.

2. Avoid discussing politics or sensitive topics unless you have a close relationship with the person you're speaking to.

3. Don't point with your index finger; it is considered impolite. Instead, use your whole hand or nod in the direction you want to indicate.

4. Avoid excessive public displays of affection, as Greeks tend to be more reserved in public.

5. Don't expect shops or restaurants to be open during siesta hours (usually from 2 pm to 5 pm). Plan your activities accordingly.

6. Avoid haggling or negotiating prices in stores unless it is explicitly indicated as acceptable.

7. Refrain from touching or removing items from archaeological sites or historical landmarks. Respect their cultural significance.

8. Avoid stepping on the Greek flag, as it is considered disrespectful.

9. Don't drink alcohol excessively or engage in rowdy behavior, especially in public places.

10. Avoid wearing revealing or skimpy clothing when visiting religious sites or monasteries.

Remember, these are general guidelines based on local customs and etiquette in Milos, Greece. It's always a good idea to observe and adapt to the specific cultural norms and practices of the destination you're visiting to show respect and foster positive interactions with the local community.

Travel scams and how to avoid them

While Milos, Greece is generally a safe destination, it's always wise to be aware of potential travel scams that can occur in any tourist destination. Here are some common travel scams and tips on how to avoid them:

1. Taxi Overcharging: Some taxi drivers may try to overcharge tourists, especially if they sense that you're unfamiliar with the area. To avoid this, always ask for an estimated fare before getting into a taxi or use a reputable taxi service. Additionally, consider using ride-hailing apps to ensure transparency in pricing.

2. Fake Tickets and Guided Tours: Be cautious when purchasing tickets or booking guided tours from street vendors or unknown sources. Stick to reputable travel agencies or purchase tickets directly from official websites. Research and read reviews before booking any tours to ensure they are legitimate.

3. Street Vendors and Pushy Salespeople: In popular tourist areas, you may encounter street vendors or salespeople who aggressively try to sell you various items or services. It's best to politely decline their offers and keep walking. Avoid engaging in conversations or accepting unsolicited help from strangers.

4. Restaurant Scams: Some restaurants may try to overcharge or add additional items to your bill, especially if they target tourists. Check menu prices before ordering and review your bill carefully before paying. It's also advisable to ask locals or do research to find reputable and authentic dining establishments.

5. Distraction Theft: Be cautious of individuals who may try to distract you, either by asking for directions, spilling something on you, or causing a commotion. While you're distracted, an accomplice may attempt to steal your belongings. Keep your valuables secure and be aware of your surroundings.

6. Fake Police Officers: Beware of individuals posing as police officers who ask to see your identification or search your belongings. Ask for proper identification and, if you're unsure, inform them that you'll contact the local police station to verify their identity. It's best to report any suspicious encounters to the local authorities.

7. ATM and Credit Card Fraud: Use ATMs located in well-lit and secure areas, preferably within banks. Shield your PIN when entering it, and be cautious of individuals who may try to watch or distract you. Regularly check your credit card and bank statements for any unauthorized charges.

8. Charity Scams: Be wary of individuals or groups soliciting donations for charities or causes. If you wish to contribute, consider donating to well-established organizations directly rather than giving money to individuals on the street.

To avoid falling victim to travel scams
- Research your destination before your trip to familiarize yourself with common scams.

- Use reputable travel services, accommodations, and tour operators.

- Keep your personal belongings secure, using hotel safes or secure bags.

- Trust your instincts and be cautious of overly friendly or aggressive individuals.

- Be aware of your surroundings and stay vigilant in crowded or touristy areas.

By staying informed, exercising caution, and being aware of potential scams, you can have a safer and more enjoyable travel experience in Milos, Greece.

Essential Phrases in Greek

Learning a few basic phrases in Greek can greatly enhance your experience in Milos, Greece. While many locals speak English, making an effort to communicate in their native language is always appreciated. Here are some essential phrases to help you navigate and interact with the locals:

1. Hello: Γεια σας (Yah-sas)

2. Good morning: Καλημέρα (Kaliméra)

3. Good evening: Καλησπέρα (Kalispera)

4. Goodbye: Αντίο (Adío)

5. Please: Παρακαλώ (Parakaló)

6. Thank you: Ευχαριστώ (Efcharistó)

7. Yes: Ναι (Ne)

8. No: Όχι (Óhi)

9. Excuse me: Συγνώμη (Signómi)

10. Sorry: Λυπάμαι (Lypámai)

11. Do you speak English?: Μιλάτε αγγλικά; (Miláte angliká?)

12. I don't understand: Δεν καταλαβαίνω (Den katalavéno)

13. Help: Βοήθεια (Voítheia)

14. Where is...?: Πού είναι...; (Pú íne...?)

15. How much does it cost?: Πόσο κοστίζει; (Póso kostízi?)

16. Can you recommend a good restaurant?: Μπορείτε να προτείνετε ένα καλό εστιατόριο; (Boríte na protínete éna kaló estiatório?)

17. I would like...: Θα ήθελα... (Tha íthela...)

18. Cheers!: Υγεία (Yiá sas)

19. Where is the bathroom?: Πού είναι η τουαλέτα; (Pú íne ee tu-a-lé-ta?)

20. Can you help me with directions?: Μπορείτε να με βοηθήσετε με τις οδηγίες; (Boríte na me voithísete me tis odigíes?)

Remember, making an effort to speak even a few basic phrases in Greek shows respect and can go a long way in building rapport with the locals. Don't be afraid to try, and most importantly, enjoy your interactions with the warm and friendly people of Milos!

Conclusion

In conclusion, Milos, Greece, is a captivating destination that offers a unique blend of natural beauty, cultural heritage, and warm hospitality. This travel guide has provided comprehensive information and insights to help you make the most of your visit to this enchanting island.

From the awe-inspiring landscapes of Sarakiniko Beach and the hidden gems of Pollonia, to the archaeological wonders of the Ancient Theatre and the tranquil fishing village of Klima, Milos offers a diverse range of attractions and activities to suit every traveler's interests.

Exploring the island's rich history and cultural heritage through its museums, ancient sites, and traditional festivals allows you to connect with the island's past and gain a deeper understanding of its unique character.

Indulging in the local cuisine, savoring the flavors of fresh seafood and traditional Greek dishes, and sampling the renowned Milos wines adds a delicious culinary dimension to your journey.

Engaging in outdoor adventures like hiking, scuba diving, and windsurfing allows you to experience the island's natural wonders and adrenaline-pumping activities.

As you immerse yourself in the local customs and traditions, you'll discover the warmth and friendliness of the Milos people, adding a personal touch to your travel experience.

Remember to plan your trip carefully, taking into account the best time to visit, essential packing items, and safety tips to ensure a smooth and enjoyable journey.

Whether you're seeking relaxation, adventure, cultural exploration, or a combination of them all, Milos has something special to offer. Let this travel guide be your companion as you embark on an unforgettable journey to this hidden gem of the Aegean.

Embrace the beauty, embrace the culture, and embrace the spirit of Milos, Greece. Bon voyage!